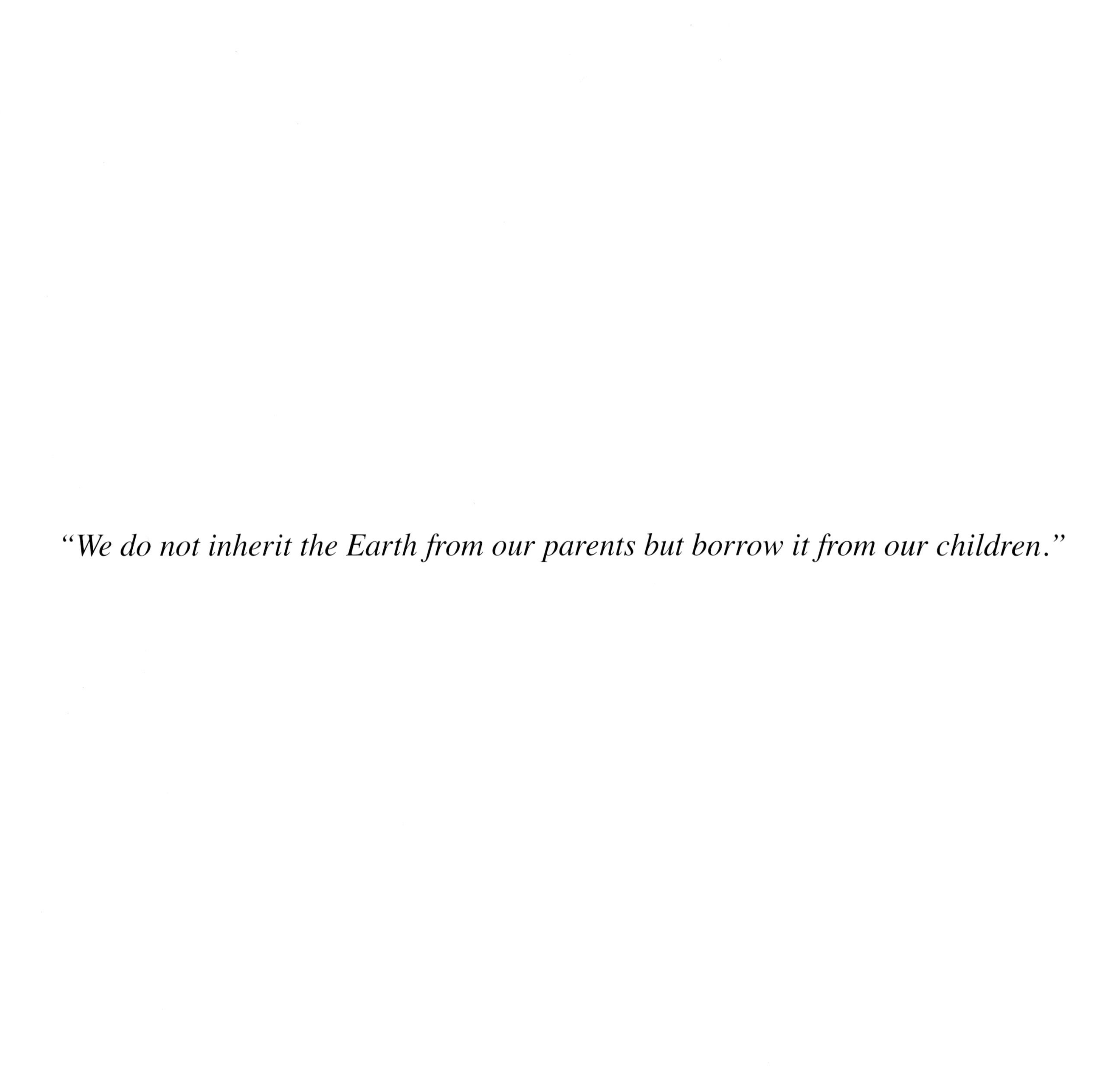

"We do not inherit the Earth from our parents but borrow it from our children."

OVERSIZE

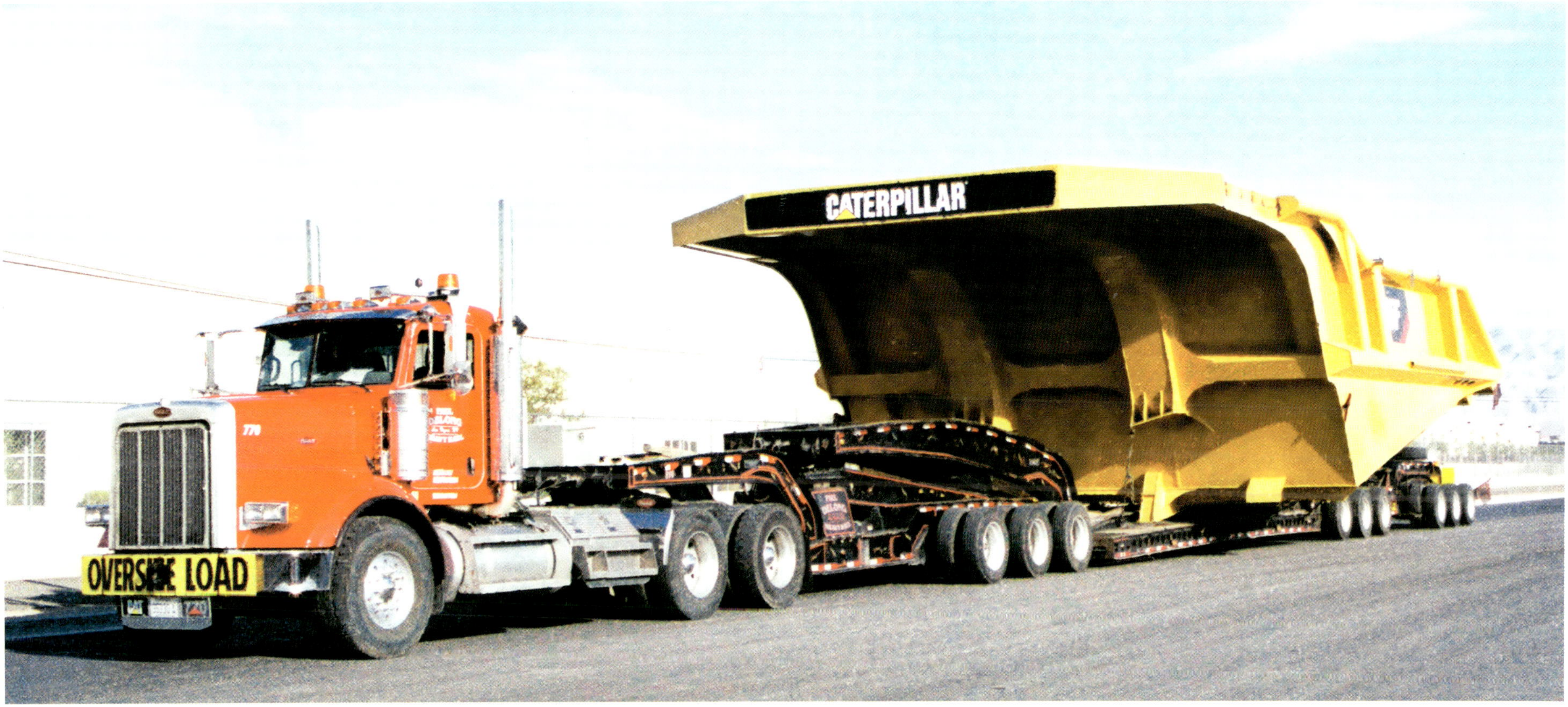

Images of Heavy Western Trucking, Vol. 1

By Mark Wayman

Dedication

I would like to dedicate this book to the memory of my first wife Terri Lynne Wayman, 3/31/56 - 3/2/2001. She was my partner, my wife and my best friend. She blessed my life with her love, her patience and her compassion. She also blessed me with two fine sons, David William and Jared Mark. She was truly an angel while she was with us and in leaving us she taught us the true meaning of faith, hope and love.
I would also like to remember my father and my mother, Ken and Ruth Wayman. It is because of their love, encouragement, support and sacrifice that their children were able to "reach for the stars" and pursue and achieve their artistic endeavors.
Lastly, I would like to thank my high school music teacher, Raymond Henderson for helping me to understand that even when we grow up we still learn lessons from those much wiser than we!

"FAITH, HOPE AND LOVE, BUT THE GREATEST OF THESE IS LOVE"

ISBN-13: 978-0-9843442-0-8

Printed in China

Cover and book design by Shawn Lewis
Copyediting by Shawn Lewis

Published by:
Buffalo Road Imports, LLC
10120 Main Street
Clarence, NY 14031, USA

In Memoriam

Gheral Brownlow, Joe Corey, Henry Davis, Robert Delgadillo, William Dey, Bill Goddard, Bob Goerke, Don Hartman, Stan Holtzman, Ben Karlsen, Howard Knighten, Kirk Knighten, Bob Lienbach, Cecil Pelts, Dee Powers, Bob Rzasa, Edgar Rojas, Dick Ryan, Tom Starks, George Thomson and Don Wood

Credits:

Front Cover: The ground shakes as 636hp roar from under the hood of the big white Mack prime mover as it assaults the grade with its heavy OVERSIZE load. A Kenworth W900 with 400 additional horsepower is shoving hard on the rear of this 255 foot long consist. Nestled between the "Dual Lane" trailer's 100 foot long main support beams is a 495,000 pound transformer. This heavy over dimensional load is riding on 128 tires as it travels the 17 mile distance from a rail siding at Railroad Pass to the Eldorado power plant.

Frontispiece: A Dielco Crane Service Manitowoc 2250 lifts a 500,000 pound jet turbine high above Pan Western Heavy Haul's Trail King TK550 suspension beam heavy haul trailer. Truck #1023 spots it's consist under the 2250 which will place the turbine inside the TK550 beam rails so that the turbine can be transported to a new gas fired electric power plant. Truck #1023 is a 2002 Kenworth T800W which is equipped with a 550hp Cat C15 diesel, an 18 speed transmission, a 2 speed auxiliary transmission and Sisu high speed planetary rear ends. Pan Western Corporation of Las Vegas, Nevada has been serving the great southwest with specialized truck transportation service since 1970 and has been in the specialized over dimensional transportation business since 2001.

Title Page: The bed from a Cat 795 rock truck rides on a Paul DeLong Heavy Haul 12 axle lowbed truck and trailer combination. Up front is truck #770, a 2007 Peterbilt 357 heavy haul truck tractor with a 550hp Cat C15 diesel, an 18 speed transmission with a 4 speed auxiliary transmission and 52,000 pound rear ends. A Cozad 3+3+3 heavy haul lowbed trailer follows #770 with its impressive OVERSIZE load.

Back Cover (top): Two Robinson Transport coal trains await their next call to work. Robinson Transport of Salina, Utah operates 75 matched sets of aluminum Beall Trailer Silver Bullets which are all dedicated to hauling coal to Intermountain power plants. Kenworth W900B truck tractors provide the power to move these impressive OVERSIZE Rocky Mountain Doubles.

Back Cover (bottom): 1000hp from this Payhauler prime mover roar to life as the sun rises at Dry Lake, Nevada. Bragg Crane #2 will soon be on the move transporting its OVERSIZE load, a transformer that is loaded on its 12 line Goldhofer platform trailer, to the new substation located at Crystal, Nevada.

Contents

A 163,000 pound Terex HC 210 crawler crane rides on an Empire Transport 10 axle heavy haul truck with trailer combination. Truck #9942 is a 1996 Kenworth T800W which is equipped with a 550hp Cat 3406E diesel, an 18 speed transmission and dual speed 46,000 pound rear ends. The 2+2+2 heavy haul lowbed trailer was manufactured by Trail King Industries of Mitchell, South Dakota. Empire Transport of Mesa, Arizona was founded in 1974 and serves the continental United Sates with 51 trucks dedicated to serving the needs of specialized transportation customers. Empire Transport is a division of Empire Southwest Inc.

Acknowledgements

First of all and foremost, I need to thank Brandon Lewis and Shawn Lewis of Buffalo Road Imports for allowing this dream to come to fruition. This book would not have been possible without the backing and support of Brandon Lewis who not only published this book but also allowed me to have input into its conception, development, editing and final rendition. This book would also not have been possible without the efforts of my close friend Shawn Lewis. While it is I who had the privilege and the pleasure to photo document the subjects in this book, it is Shawn who had to perform the brutally tedious tasks of sorting and scanning the images, making sense of my notes and editing the text. I am quite sure that Shawn had a lot more hair on his head before he tackled this project.

This book is only possible because of the generosity and kindness that was extended to me by Arnold Braasch of Renssalaer, Indiana and Richard "Dick" Dieleman of Boulder City, Nevada. They always found the time to answer my questions, to offer their opinion, their advice, their assistance and to help me to gain access to places that I never imagined existed. I am fortunate to have made not only their acquaintance but also their friendship.

I need to thank the following friends for not only their time but also their interest and their assistance in helping me to make this book possible, Darrell Dieleman, David Dieleman, Roger Dieleman, Billy Cunningham and Clif Blanc all from Dielco Crane Service. Chuck Beam, Paul Delong, Joe Manley, Ron Bunker, Earl Sutton, Brad Sutton, Larry Littrell, Buddy Pelts, Stacy Bettridge, Tracy Harris, Mike Branson, Ralph Johnson, Richard Mark, Ed Sweeney, Paul Morton, Francis Pierre, Moe Truman, Matt Listro, Carl Cunningham and Dennis Haun.

I also need to recognize and thank the following two friends, Stephen Lynn Peters not only for his friendship, but for the countless hours spent driving on photographic adventures and also for the many, many hours spent in his dark room sharing with me and teaching me "The Master's Secrets". Joe McMillan who set a standard for telephoto photography that to this day has still only been copied and seldom equaled.

The following people contributed their time and furnished information for this book. In alphabetical order:
Trip Aiken, Dennis Almas, Clayton Alvey, Harvey Bailey, Dan Bulloch, Wayne Calder, D.E. Chambers, Wes Chandler, Lynn Cusey, Don Denman, Jerome Dey, Jesse Dey, Matthew Dey, David Faust, Mike Fish, Justin Gilmet, Dan Goins, Lynn Goodfellow, Ken Groves, Mark Heinz, Don Helm, Dan Horlacher, J. Arnold Horne, Keith Jackson, Randy Keller, Paul Knowles, Mark Lavery, Paul Leavitt, Randy Ledermann, Don Miller, Gary Morton, Dave Natale, Butch Odegaard, Jim Orr, Milo Palmer, Gene Pasini, Wes Paulson, Jim Pennington, Liz Petrillo, Patti Pierce, Dennis Poland, Don Poppe, Mike Poppe, Tyronne Powledge, Kim Robinson, Lee Robinson, Scott Robinson, Frank Romo, Darrell Shaw, Chris Sissick, David Soriano, Dan Spaulding, Hank Suderman, Pat Turner, Dale Wagner, Mike Wantland, Terry Warner, Tim Washburn, Alan Weddle, Bobby Weyers, Marc Williams, Ed Wright and John Yusunas.

Introduction

OVERSIZE is photo gallery of over dimensional loads that move throughout the Western United States. Over dimension loads are normally overwidth loads, overheight loads, overlength loads or overweight loads. This book features some of the trucks, trailers and equipment that are needed to move these over dimensional loads. This book also features some of the companies who operate the specialized equipment needed to complete the job safely, conomically and on schedule.

Specialized transportation equipment is engineered, designed and fabricated to meet the needs and requirements of each particular job. The equipment is also designed to meet the very stringent and complex "bridge laws" for each state that the specialized transportation contractor operates in. These "bridge laws" are used to calculate the formulas that allow maximum weight per axle that carry the load. The manufacturers who build the trucks, trailers and equipment design their products to evenly distribute the weight of the payload so that the specialized transportation contractors can legally meet the various state bridge law requirements.

Some over dimensional movements require years of engineered planning and not only deal with the logistics of moving the specialized cargo but may also deal with interstate transportation of the cargo as well as the permitting that is required move that load in the individual states involved.

The commitment to safety is priority number 1 when it comes to the operation of their over dimensional equipment and the specialized transportation companies that operate throughout the Western United States maintain a maintenance schedule that keeps their equipment "show room new". The maintenance and TLC that this equipment receives is unequaled in the transportation industry and many pieces of equipment serve their owners for 30 years or more.

The trucks in this book are not the "glamor girls" that sparkle and shine as they travel the Western United States. The trucks in this book work and perform under the most demanding schedules and in unforgiving environments. They perform in the sun, the rain, the sleet, the mud and the snow. They perform in the heat, the cold and the wind.

The trucks in this book are truly an awesome sight to behold as they earn their keep safely moving heavy OVERSIZE loads to their final destination.

This Mack CH613 super tanker wears the very appealing silver and red over black corporate paint scheme of Texaco USA. Power for the black Bulldog that pulls the matched pair of polished aluminum Heil tank trailers comes from a 454hp Mack E7 diesel which has been mated to a 10 speed transmission.

Super Heavy Haul

Large over dimensional loads need specialized equipment to transport them. These loads require multiple axle combinations to evenly distribute the weight load and carry it safely.

The triangular "cut outs" in the trailer frame rails identify this 150 ton dual lane heavy haul trailer as a Trail King TK 300. Pulling the TK 300 is Vosburg Equipment truck #165, a brand new 1996 Kenworth T800W. With 2 speed rear ends and an 18 speed transmission, the big KW's 455hp Cat 3406E diesel will have no problems moving this 180,000 pound transformer 17 miles up the road to a new "gas fired" power plant.

This big blue Bulldog prime mover belongs to Van Dyke Brothers, Inc. of Chandler, Minnesota. #2 is a 1986 Mack RD-866SX and was delivered new with a 998 cubic inch 500hp E-9 Mack power plant, a 12 speed transmission, a 4 speed auxiliary transmission and 65,000 rear ends. The Bulldog's drive train is very well suited to handle the Trail King TS 580 suspension beam trailer with its transformer load. Van Dyke Brother's have been handling heavy oversize loads for over 40 years.

Christened "Big Country", this awesome red, white and blue 1000hp Kenworth 6X6 prime mover is one truly impressive piece of machinery. Big Country was conceived and designed by the owner of American Heavy Moving and Rigging. The truck's main components and sub assemblies were delivered to American's shop in Chino, California where the truck was meticulously assembled and finished. Power for this big Kenworth comes from a twin turbo Cat 3412 diesel. A Clark 8 speed automatic transmission supplies torque to the three 91,000 pound Clark planetary drive axles. A Tulsa 100,000 pound winch sits upon the deck behind the cab. A 430,000 pound transformer sits suspended between the 85 foot long beams of the trailer. This beam trailer rides on two sets of dual tandem beams, front and back, which are supported by 12 dollies and a total of 96 tires. The total length of the rig, from front bumper to rear of push truck is 264 feet. The push trucks bringing up the rear are #19 and #20, both 2000 Kenworth T800W's. Under the hoods are Cat's big 600hp C16 diesel engines which deliver traction to the dual speed 52,000 pound rear axles through an 18 speed transmission. American Heavy Moving and Rigging has been in business since 1981. For the past 28 years American has built a solid reputation for their ability to move safely and efficiently the most difficult of projects.

With a 27,000 ballast box for added traction Bragg Crane #2 backs it's 12 line Goldhofer platform trailer up a heavy wooden matt ramp so that it's transformer load can be "jacked, rolled and set" on a concrete pad. Bragg Crane #2 is a 1975 Payhauler 350. In 1980, Bragg Crane purchased two very used Payhaulers from a local aggregate quarry. They had their dump beds removed and they were completely overhauled and rebuilt, from the frame up, by Bragg in their Long Beach, California shops where they were converted to prime movers #1 and #2. They both have 1000hp Cummins V12 diesel motors which are coupled to Allison 5 speed automatic transmissions. They are also both equipped with retarders and double reduction all wheel drive planetaries. Bragg Crane was founded in Southern California in 1946 and today, Bragg maintains facilities in California, Nevada and Arizona. For over 60 years the Bragg Companies have offered their customers heavy lift, heavy transportation and rigging services. The heavy duty Goldhofer modular trailer was manufactured in Germany and as configured has 96 tires to help evenly distribute the weight of its heavy oversize load.

Heavy Transport HT100 is a 1988 Peterbilt 379. A 475hp Cat 3406B provides power to dual speed 42,000 pound rear ends through a 16 speed transmission. BRAGG 2, a 75,000 pound Payhauler prime mover sits on the deck of Siebert 2+2+2 lowbed heavy haul trailer. Heavy Transport is the heavy haul and specialized transportation division of Bragg Crane. Siebert trailers were manufactured in Stockton, California from the mid 1970's until 1991 when they were absorbed by Kalyn Industries forming Kalyn Siebert Trailers of Gatesville, Texas.

Truck #370 is 2006 Kenworth T800W. #370 was delivered with a 550hp Cat C15 diesel motor. An 18 speed transmission delivers power to a pair of Sisu high speed planetary rear axles.

Truck #362P is a 1981 Peterbilt 387 with a 435hp Cummins motor, 18 speed transmission and 91,000 pound planetary rear ends.

Sunrise at Vidal Junction, California finds Intermountain Rigging and Heavy Haul's massive Trail King dual lane beam trailer loaded with a 360,000 pound autoclave bound for a copper mine at Morenci, Arizona. The autoclave is the last of two that were manufactured in Pocatello, Idaho and transported the 1568 mile long journey by Intermountain Rigging and Heavy Haul. IRH has installed their extended suspension beams to accommodate the length of the load which allows a total of 128 tires to safely move it. The total length from front bumper to the second push truck's rear end is 360 feet. Truck #370 is 2006 Kenworth T800W. #370 was delivered with a 550hp Cat C15 diesel motor. An 18 speed transmission delivers power to a pair of Sisu high speed planetary rear axles. Supplying power to the rear of the trailer is an additional 910 horsepower. Truck #362P is a 1981 Peterbilt 387 with a 435hp Cummins motor, 18 speed transmission and 91,000 pound planetary rear ends. Truck #361 is a 1993 Kenworth W900B with a 475hp Cat motor, 18 speed transmission with a 2 speed auxiliary transmission. Intermountain Rigging & Heavy Haul was formed in 1997 when Intermountain Rigging & Transfer merged with Savage Industries Heavy Haul Division, both of Salt Lake City, Utah.

MACK
Mack
BIGGE
BIGGE
BIGGE
BPM-1
OVERSIZE LOAD
BIGGE
BIGGE

Having just crossed the bridge spanning the mighty Colorado River at Needles, California, 2 Bigge Crane and Rigging prime movers move this power plant sub assembly into Arizona. This unit is over 255 feet long and is riding on a total of 146 tires.

Up front is Bigge BPM1, a 1977 Mack M-45SX. The drive train components include a 636hp 16V71 Detroit Diesel, a 6 speed Allison 6061 automatic transmission and 120,000 pound Mack planetary rear ends.

Bringing up the rear is BPM3, an 8X8 Ward LaFrance M-746 that was acquired by Bigge in 2000. BPM3's drive train components include a twin turbo 475hp 8V92TTA Detroit Diesel and a 5 speed Twin Disc automatic transmission with retarder.

Originally founded in Northern California's Bay area by Henry Bigge in 1916 as Bigge Drayage Company, Bigge Crane and Rigging is today one of the nation's largest specialized service companies.

OVERSIZE LOAD

This 350 ton Nicolas suspension beam trailer belongs to Reliance Crane & Rigging of Phoenix, Arizona. A 350,000 pound HRSG super heater bundle rests inside the beam rails. The massive twin steer Mack prime mover is one of two that were completely rebuilt at the Reliance shop facility. Both Mack prime movers, PM #1 and PM #2, have two heavy 24,000 pound front axles, 636hp Cummins diesels, 6 speed Allison automatic transmissions and 120,000 pound rear ends. Reliance also fabricated and installed the completely new cowls and side mount cabs.

A KW Dart 55 ton prime mover is coupled to the rear of the Nicolas trailer. The KW Dart is also one of two prime movers that were completely rebuilt at the Reliance shops. The traditional rock truck cabs were removed and new side mount cabs were installed on both PM #7 and PM #8. Both KW Darts also have 636hp Cummins diesels, 6 speed Allison automatic transmissions and 130,000 pound rear ends. The trailer and the front and rear load spreading platform beams were built by Nicolas Industries of France. There are 144 tires supporting the trailer.

Reliance Crane Rental began as Reliance Truck in 1935. Reliance Crane Rental was established in 1968.

Riding on 64 tires, a 350,000 pound HRSG super heater "bundle" sits on a custom fabricated frame rail trailer that was built by Shaughnessy Heavy Industries of Auburn, Washington. The "bundle" was transloaded from rail car to the trailer for delivery to a power plant in the Eldorado Valley. Providing power for this movement is H4, a 1987 Freightliner. The drive train for H4 includes a 400hp Cat 3406E diesel motor, a Fuller 1208LL, an 8 speed transmission with a 4 speed Spicer auxiliary transmission and 46,000 pound rear ends. H9, a 1981 Kenworth W900 is attached to rear of the trailer supplying an additional 400 horse power to help move the bundle set to its destination.

Shaughnessy and Company has been providing heavy haul transportation and rigging to the Pacific Northwest, Western Canada and Alaska since 1909.

Arriving from the manufacturer by rail car, these HRSG's, heat recovery steam generators, have been spotted on the loading track under the heavy lift gantry where they will be trans loaded from the rail car by Shaughnessy Heavy Industries to a specially designed 64 tire frame trailer and transported to the power plant job site.

ERSIZE LOAD
223

Southwest Industrial Rigging's 15 line Goldhofer trailer sits at Abra, Arizona where the 275,000 pound transformer it carries was transloaded from a rail car for movement to a substation at Prescott, 20 miles away. Pulling the Goldhofer trailer is #223, a 2000 Peterbilt 379. The sharp looking Pete is powered by a 550hp Cat diesel coupled to an 18 speed transmission that drives the dual speed 46,000 pound rear ends. Southwest Industrial Rigging has been in business serving Arizona and the Great South West for 28 years. The Goldhofer platform trailer was manufactured in Germany.

Almas International's prime mover #135 prepares to move an airplane hangar to a new location. Built in Canada in 1976, this magnificent Pacific P-12W3 6X6 was delivered with a powerful drive train that includes a 600hp Cummins KTA diesel, a heavy duty Allison 5 speed automatic transmission, a 24,000 pound front drive axle and 121,000 pound planetary rear ends.

Almas International started out in Southern California in 1933 as Almas Brothers House Moving. Over the years they built a solid reputation for their abilities to move not only homes and buildings but also challenging heavy loads. Almas International was formed in 1965 as the company expanded its services to meet the needs of customers worldwide.

In 1988 Jake's Crane, Rigging and Transport designed, fabricated and assembled, in their Las Vegas, Nevada shop facilities, a modular super heavy haul transport system that would allow heavy load equalization through the use of a hydraulic nitrogen suspension system. The JXS, "Jake's Xtra Speed," was an ultra heavy haul transport system that was designed to meet the stringent California DOT bridge weight formulas by evenly distributing payload and maximizing gross weight efficiency. The JXS system was also deigned to handle and move loads of up to 250 tons at highway speeds.

Assembled with a set of suspension beams, the JXS modular transport system rests for the night as it awaits its predawn safety inspections before continuing on its journey to deliver its 262,000 pound transformer load to a coal fired power plant. Riding on a total of 90 tires, the total length of this rig from front bumper to rear of pusher truck is 200 feet.

Sitting up front is truck #385, quite possibly the most famous of all west coast heavy haul Peterbilt truck tractors. New in 1985, this truly awesome Peterbilt 359 was assembled with an 1150 cubic inch 600hp Cummins KTA series diesel motor, a 15 speed transmission and dual speed 52,000 pound rear ends. #385 would perform so flawlessly under strenuous load hauling conditions that in 1987 a twin unit was delivered, #387. Handling the rear end is a heavy haul spec'd Peterbilt 362 COE, #388. Purchased new in 1988, #388 was delivered with a 460hp "N" series Cummins diesel motor, a 15 speed transmission and 48,000 pound dual speed rear ends.

Jake's Crane was founded in 1946 and continues today to serve the specialized needs of the crane, rigging and transportation industries.

JAKE'S
RIGGING
(702)736-4082
LIC 1121.A.B(NV)
ICC MC1547345
CPC A2373(NV)
OVERSIZE LOAD

Contractor's Cargo started out in 1933 with one truck serving the Southern California area. Today, Contractor's Cargo operates 26 Kenworth heavy haul truck tractors out of their Compton, California and Houston, Texas terminals. Contractor's Cargo specializes in Heavy Haul Transportation, Erecting and Rigging. They offer their services throughout the continental United States as well as Canada and Mexico.

Loaded on the deck of their 16 axle Peerless trailer is a 157,000 pound Toshiba steam generator. Truck #83 is a 2006 Kenworth T800W. An ISX 500hp Cummins diesel supplies power to an 18 speed transmission which is coupled to a 2 speed auxiliary transmission. This particular truck is one of 4 that are equipped with a lift axle. All four of these units are based in Houston. Peerless Trailers was started in 1944 in Portland Oregon. Today, Peerless continues to build specialized trailers and equipment to meet the needs of the construction, logging and oil exploration industries.

Contractors Cargo Co.
Contractors Cargo Co.
Contractors Cargo Co.
OVERSIZE LOA

DO NOT HUMP
DO NOT HUMP
DAVENPORT MAMMOET
584
MAM ET
DIESEL

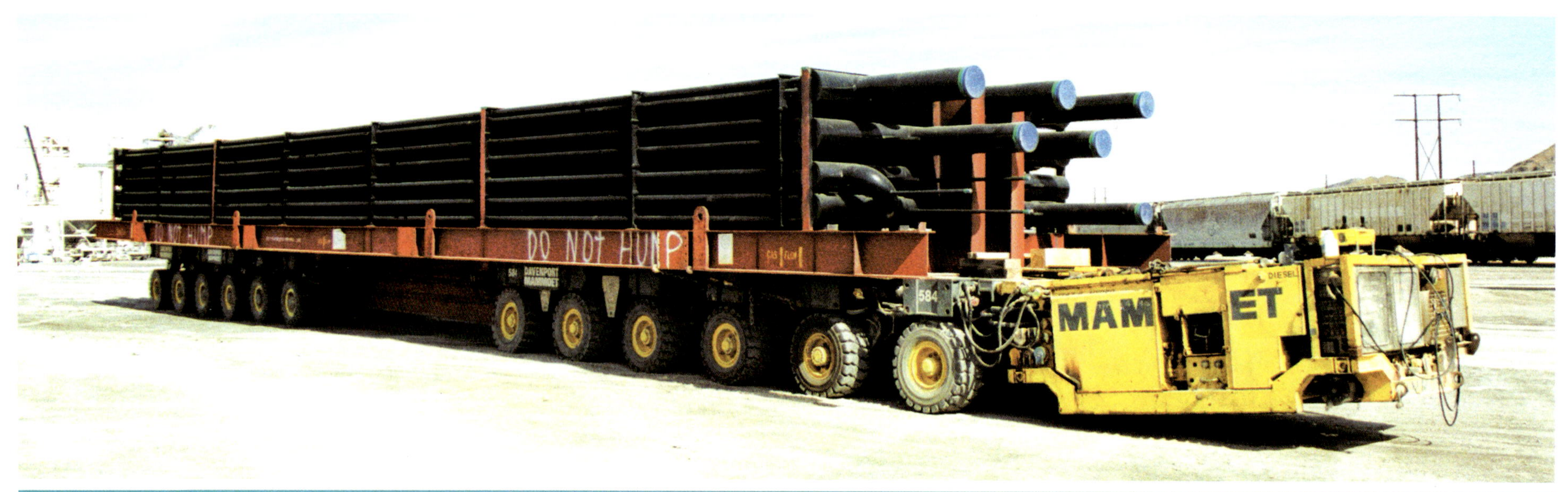

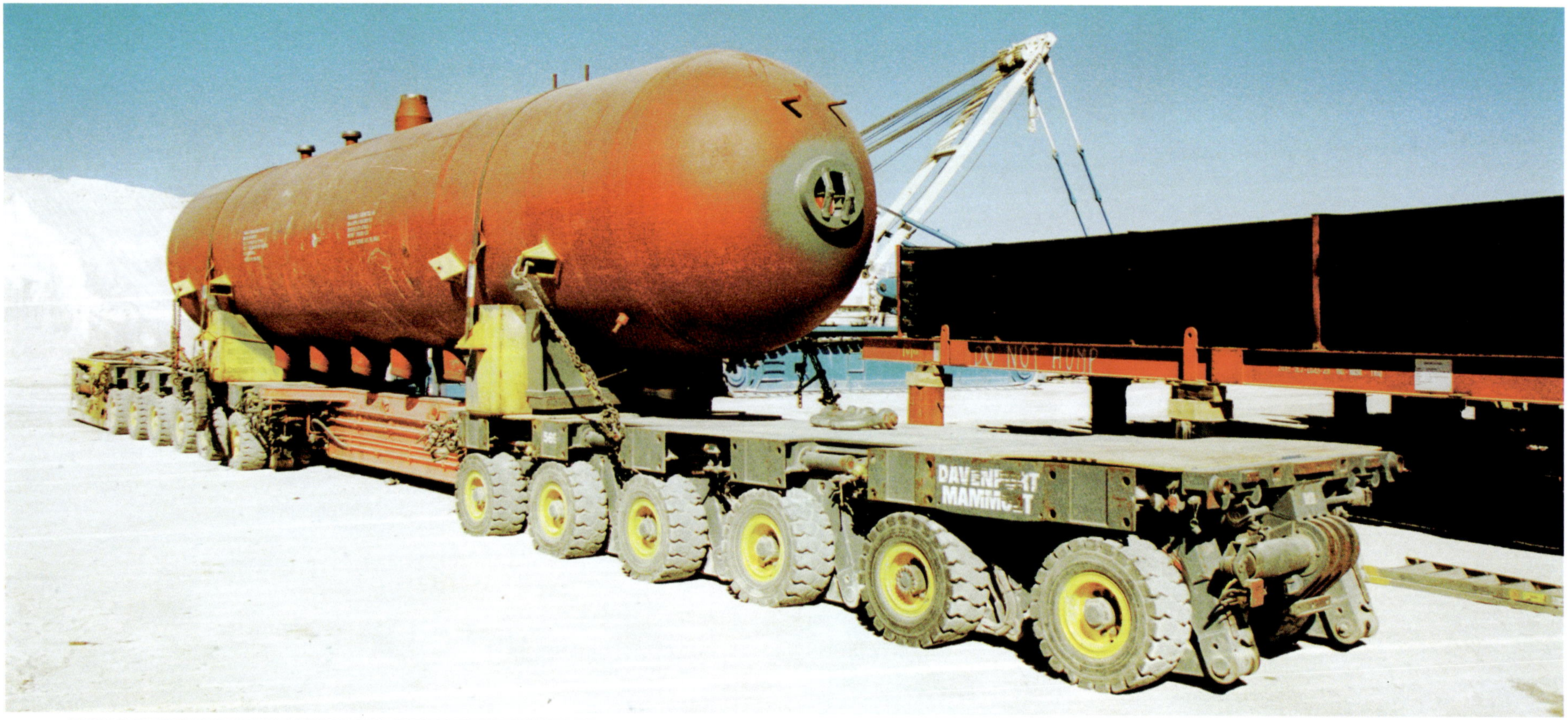
DO NOT HUMP
DAVENPORT MAMMOET

This Scheuerle Self Propelled Modular Transporter (SPMT) has been loaded with a HRSG (Heat Recovery Steam Generator). The SPMT will transport the super heater "bundle" on a private haul road to a new gas fired electric power plant. The SPMT belongs to Mammoet USA which was formed as a separate operating division of Mammoet Holding BV in 2000. Mammoet provides specialized services worldwide that include crane, rigging, heavy lift, heavy transport and salvage at sea. Scheuerle, of Pfedelbach, Germany was founded in1869 and today is the world's largest manufacturer of heavy duty transporters. They manufacture specialized transportation vehicles that can carry from 15 to 15,000 tons.

OVERSIZE LOAD

A 250,000 pound HRSG super heater "bundle" rides inside a Pan Western Trail King TK 450 heavy haul suspension beam trailer. Up front a 550hp Kenworth T800W heavy haul truck tractor leads it's consist as it approaches its destination, an under construction gas fired electric power plant, while a 550hp Kenworth T800W tri drive heavy haul tractor is pushing hard at the rear.
Once inside the gates of the power plant the rear truck will be uncoupled from the TK450 so that the "bundle" can be lifted out and then installed into the tower.

Pan Western's truck #57, a Peterbilt 379 heavy haul truck tractor, has its assignment under control as it slowly eases its Trail King TK550 suspension beam trailer under a 500,000 pound generator stator that has been suspended for "load out" by a heavy lift gantry. Once the stator has been loaded between the suspension beam rails, the OVERSIZE load will ride on the TK 550's 96 tires to its delivery destination.

Long recognized as a leader in the drill shaft industry, Anderson Drilling has been in the ground boring business since 1945. In 1986, Anderson Manufacturing, a division of Anderson Drilling designed, fabricated and assembled two state of the art rotary drill rig units that could ride on three different carrier options. Christened "Big Stan #1" and "Big Stan #2" these massive 50 foot long drill rig frames could be mounted on either a 12 foot wide 5 axle rubber tired drill carrier chassis, a 20 foot wide crawler carrier chassis or a 12 foot half track carrier chassis.

Riding on a custom fabricated 3 axle Murray lowbed trailer is the 90 foot long drill mast for Big Stan #1. Truck #TKO1 is a 1973 Mack DMM-6966SX which has a Detroit Diesel, a 13 speed transmission and rides on twin 12,000 pound front steer axles and 55,000 pound rear ends. Anderson Drilling designed this impressive drill rig so that it could be completely set up "ready to drill" in an hour. The drill mast trailer has outriggers that enable it to lift itself up so that any one of the carriers can be backed up under the mast and easily mounted. #BS01 is a five axle 1983 Pettibone crane carrier chassis which has a 350hp Cummins diesel motor, an 8LL transmission with a 2 speed auxiliary transmission and it rides on three 22,000 pound front steer axles with 120,000 pound planetary rear drive axles. The drill rig itself has an enormous 600hp Cummins KTA diesel which supplies power to the drill shaft through an Allison 8 speed automatic transmission. Anderson Drilling operates 5 divisions which serve 14 Western States. Anderson Drilling is recognized as a leader and innovator in rock drilling, earth retention systems and large diameter access excavating.

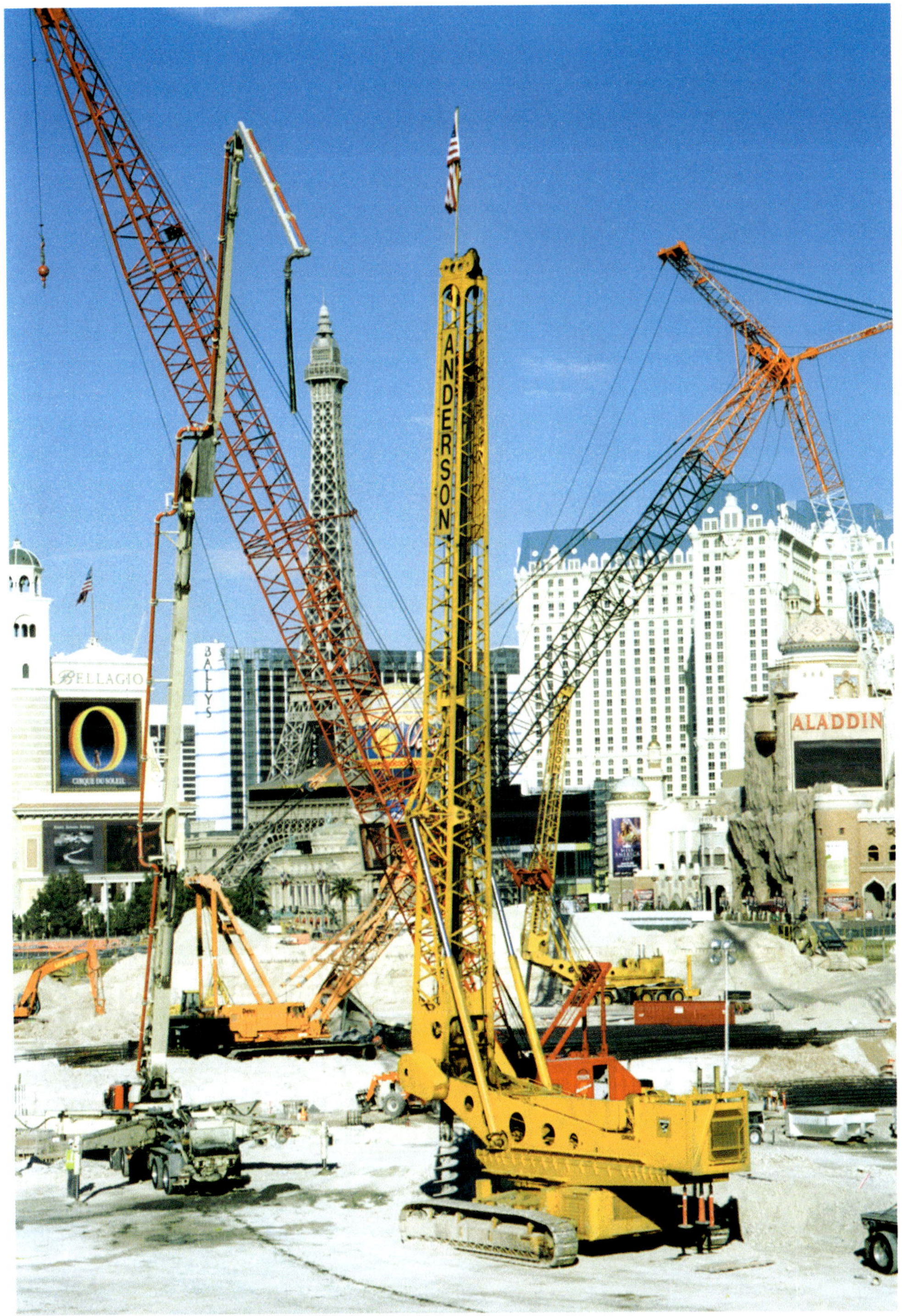
ANDERSON
BELLAGIO
ALADDIN

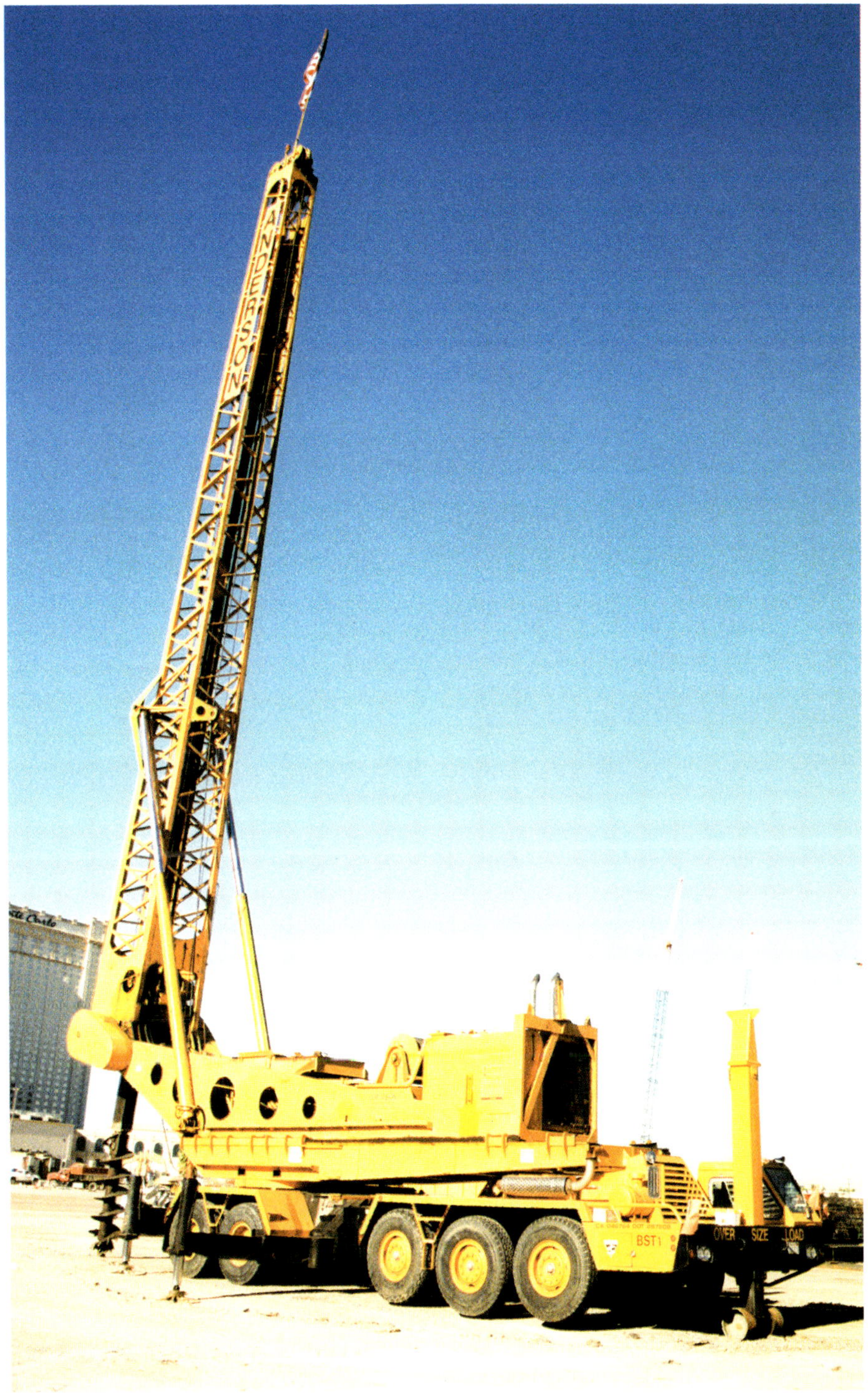
ANDERSON
OVER SIZE LOAD

An 80 ton prestressed concrete bridge girder tub beam has been loaded into a 12 foot wide 100 ton Peerless Page heavy duty heavy transport trailer. A Kenworth 848 heavy haul prime mover will position the trailer under a Strukturas overhead launching gantry so that the tub girder can be lifted and transported by the gantry through the loading truss system for placement and final connection. The truss system can reach a total length of over 780 feet if needed and can articulate 20 degrees at each end. The prime mover has a "Buzzin Dozen" 525hp Detroit V-12 diesel, a 13 speed main transmission with a 4 speed auxiliary transmission and 91,000 pound Clark planetary rear ends. Peerless Page has been serving the needs of the heavy logging and construction industries of Canada since 1972. Their design and manufacturing facilities are located in Penticton, British Columbia.

The Strukturas overhead launching gantry was designed and built in Norway and is being used by Walter SCI Construction Company of Toronto, Canada. A 250 ton Dielco Crane Service Link Belt 268 truck crane lifts the launching gantry for placement and installation into the truss placement system.

Overlength

Loads that exceed the maximum legal length law for one trailer are considered overlength. These loads require job specific specialized transport equipment.

S&T Trucking #111 is a 2009 Kenworth T800W that has a 115 foot long prestressed concrete girder bridge beam loaded on its 16 tire Cozad jeep and 32 tire rear steerable dolly configuration. S&T removed the 24 foot deck from their Cozad 2+2+2 heavy haul lowbed trailer to utilize the jeep and dolly in this configuration. The classy big wide nose Kenworth has a 600hp Cummins ISX diesel motor that is mated to an 18 speed gearbox. The dual speed rear ends are rated at 46,000 pounds. S&T Trucking is based out of Ranchester, Wyoming and has been in the heavy haul transportation business since 1977.

V. Van Dyke truck #141 delivers one of sixty-four 115 foot long trapezoidal tub girder bridge beams that will span the Colorado River high above Black Canyon at Hoover Dam. The tub beams were manufactured by American Bridge Company of Portland, Oregon and transported to Nevada by V. Van Dyke Inc. of Seattle, Washington.

Truck #141 is a 2007 Kenworth T800 which is equipped with a 550hp Cat C15 diesel, an 18 speed transmission and 48,000 pound rear ends. Both the trailer and the trailer dolly were manufactured by V. Van Dyke who has been in the specialized transportation business since 1950. A Mi-Jack Travelift rubber tire gantry crane unloads #141.

A 118 foot long 165,000 pound precast AASHTO concrete bridge girder beam rides on a Williamsen Manufacturing 3 axle jeep and 6 axle self steering "manned" dolly set. The concrete girder beam was poured and cast by Eagle Precast of Salt Lake City, Utah. Supplying power to move this impressive over length load is truck #3024, a 2006 Kenworth W900B. #3024's drive train includes a 550hp Cat C15 motor, an 18 speed transmission and 46,000 pound rear ends. The Williamsen Manufacturing jeep and dolly set were specially designed, fabricated and assembled for Eagle Precast at Williamsen Manufacturing's facility at Salt Lake City, Utah. Founded in 1892, Williamsen Manufacturing is the nation's oldest trailer manufacturer and continues to be a leader in the design, fabrication and assembly of custom made trailers. Eagle Precast has been supplying concrete building components to the Rocky Mountain States and the Western United Sates since 1976.

The head end of a 115 foot long steel bridge over pass girder beam rides on a fifth wheel bolster while the rear end has been tied down to a suspended flat bed trailer. This impressive OVERLENGTH load was fabricated by Utah Pacific Bridge and Steel of Linden, Utah who has been manufacturing fabricated structural metals for over 32 years. Mountain Pacific Transport is a division of Utah Pacific Bridge and Steel that handles the transportation and delivery of the fabricated structural products. Truck #9 is a 1999 Peterbilt 379 which has been equipped with a 555hp Cat 3406E diesel, an 18 speed transmission and 46,000 pound rear ends.

Custom Fabrication

Custom built equipment that is engineered, designed and fabricated to meet specific requirements and needs of operators and transporters.

Many companies take a great deal of pride in their corporate image and appearance, which reflects their commitment to safety and maintenance. That pride in image is reflected by the sharp orange and white equipment that Dielco Crane Service has operated for the past 25 years. Riding on 42 tires, the "upper" from a Link Belt 278 truck crane sits on a custom built beam trailer that was designed, fabricated and assembled by Dielco Crane in their Las Vegas, Nevada shops. Utilizing 16 tire Cozad jeeps to start with, Dielco built three of these raised rail beam trailers to accommodate the transportation of their "self decking" Link Belt 278 cranes. The crane's upper body has 4 rotating corner jacking stands that when lowered, allow the trailer to be driven away from it and then the crane carrier can be backed under it and loaded. #382 is a 1994 Kenworth T800W equipped with a 455hp Cat 3406E which has plenty of power to move the 89,000 pound crane body upper. #382 is also equipped with an 18 speed transmission with 46,000 pound dual speed rear ends.

A 64,400 pound Manitowoc 2250 crane upper rides on a custom built 4 axle skeleton frame trailer with a two axle jeep. The distinctive bright yellow over white paint scheme belongs to Crane Service Inc. of Albuquerque, New Mexico. Also dressed in yellow and white is #2990, a 1997 Peterbilt 379. #2990 has a Cat 3406E power plant which is mated to an 18 speed transmission. Crane Service Inc. has been supplying heavy lifting, rigging and specialized heavy hauling to customers in the great southwest since 1960. Crane Service Inc. also has offices in Sweetwater and El Paso, Texas.

Truck #46, a 2004 Kenworth T800W, wears the sharp black over yellow paint scheme of Precision Heavy Haul out of Tolleson, Arizona. For more than 25 years, Precision Heavy Haul has been serving the specialized needs of its customers throughout the great Southwest. When 63 brand new coal cars needed to be transported 200 miles from a rail siding at Winslow, Arizona to a coal mine near Page, Arizona, Precision Heavy Haul designed, fabricated and built this "self loading" rail car transporter in order to facilitate the moves. This specialized trailer has a 30 ton hydraulic winch which allows a 68,000 pound aluminum coal gondola car to be loaded and unloaded with ease. The Kenworth and trailer is resting at Railhead, Arizona. The truck has a 500hp Cummins ISX motor supplying power to a 52,000 pound dual speed rear end through a Fuller "super 18 speed transmission".

Riding in a custom fabricated boat transport trailer is a small tug boat. Pulling the trailer and the tugboat is a 2003 Volvo truck tractor that is equipped with a 600hp Cummins ISX diesel and a 13 speed transmission. The truck and trailer belong to Associated Boat Transport, Inc. of Marysville, Washington. Associated Boat Transport has been moving watercraft since 1920. Today their transports operate throughout the 48 continental United States, Canada and Mexico.

Custom fabricated front and rear dollies supported this ex railroad passenger car as it was removed from its home atop a warren truss railroad bridge and transported to a storage area. An ex military M-123 was used to move the 74,000 pound load. The 10 ton Mack 6X6 was more than up to the task with its 300hp Cummins diesel, 5 speed transmission with 2 speed transfer case and a 23,000 pound triple reduction front drive axle and 65,000 pound double reduction rear ends.

A Marmon SB series conventional truck tractor pulls an exterior rocket lift vehicle for the U.S. Air Force. The trailer is used to transport missile stages and components and it's 20 tires ride on Nicolas hydraulic suspension sets. This specialized trailer transporter was designed to carry 125 tons when fully loaded. The prototype was built by Talbert Trailers of Rensselaer, Indiana in the mid 1980's and although Talbert did not get the contract to build these units at least 10 were built. The big Marmon was part of an order that was placed by the government and these were some of the last trucks built before Marmon ceased operations in 1997 after over 60 years of building custom trucks.

A massive Schramm Rotadrill drill rig rides on specially designed and fabricated 2 axle trailer equipped with a 2 axle dolly. The drill mast is 60 foot in length and is riding in the down position for transportation. Power to transport the rig is provided by an R model Mack truck tractor equipped with a Mack diesel and a Mack transmission. The Water Resources division of Layne Christensen Company owns and operates this impressive drill rig. Founded in 1812 Layne Christensen offers the nation a complete range of drilling services including water well drilling, energy drilling and mineral resources exploration. Schramm Inc. of West Chester, Pennsylvania was founded in 1900 and started manufacturing drilling equipment in 1955.

Built in 1997, a Watson 3100 rotary drill rides on a Pierce Pacific carrier chassis. It is hard to believe that this "Cadillac" of carriers is 31 years old. Drill rig #26 is owned by Allen Drilling of Las Vegas, Nevada who has been in business since 1949. The 4 axle Pierce Pacific has a 6V Detroit Diesel motor and a 5 speed main transmission with a 4 speed auxiliary transmission. The carrier chassis rides on 20,000 pound front axles and 91,000 pound Clark planetary rear axles. "#26 will not get there in a hurry but it will most definitely go over anything in its way!" Pierce Pacific Manufacturing of Portland, Oregon has been designing and building heavy duty equipment for the construction, drilling and forest harvesting industries since 1931. Their custom fabricated truck carrier chassis have been extremely popular for use as crane mount, drill mount and loader mount carriers due to their solid construction which has made them reliable and durable under the most difficult of operating conditions. Watson Inc. of Ft. Worth, Texas started developing, designing and building drill rigs in 1965.

Energy

The energy construction industry requires specialized equipment for use in the building and maintaining of the powerlines, pipelines and wind turbine farms.

ATS #41114 is operated by the Wind Energy Logistics division of Anderson Trucking Service of St. Cloud, Minnesota. Anderson trucking service has been in the specialized transportation industry since 1955. The load is a 107,000 pound wind turbine tower base section that has been loaded and secured into its specially designed Trail King Schnabel transport trailer. Pulling this 13 axle consist is a 2002 Freightliner FLD 120. Under #41114's fiber glass hood is a 475hp Cat C15 motor that is coupled to an 18 speed transmission. The bright red Freightliner has 46,000 pound rear ends.

American Transport Inc. #116001 is a 2006 Kenworth T800W that is powered by a big Cat diesel and with its 24,000 pound front axle and lift axle, it is one heavy duty heavy haul truck tractor. Sitting behind the yellow and orange tractor is a wind turbine mast section which rides on a Diamond Trailer heavy haul 3+3+3 schnabel trailer. American Transport of Pittsburg, Pennsylvania has been in the specialized transportation business since 1986. The Schnabel trailer was manufactured by Diamond Trailers of Shandon, Ohio who has been designing, fabricating and assembling specialized trailers since 1986. Diamond heavy haul trailers feature diamond shaped "cut outs" in their frame rails.

This immaculate all red 9 axle heavy haul combination belongs to Homer Mann Trucking of Sylmar, California. The 2001 Peterbilt 378 heavy haul truck tractor is powered by a drive train that includes a 550hp Cat diesel engine, an 18 speed transmission and dual speed rear ends. A 195,000 pound nacelle has been loaded upon a Murray Ambassador 2+2+2 heavy haul lowbed trailer. Homer Mann Trucking has been in business for over 60 years serving the construction and specialized heavy haul industries. For nearly 50 years Harley Murray Inc. has been designing, fabricating and assembling specialized heavy haul lowbed trailers at their facility in Stockton, California. Murray Trailers are recognized for their heavy duty, durable, light weight construction which features rectangular frame rail "cut outs".

A wind turbine tower section sits on a Kalyn Siebert 2+3+2 heavy haul trailer that is being pulled by Burkey #41104, a 2002 Peterbilt 378 heavy haul tractor. The total length from front bumper to rear of trailer is 140 feet. Power for the all black 11 axle rig comes from a 550hp Cat C15 diesel motor. #41104 has an 18 speed transmission with dual speed 46,000 pound rear ends.

Nevada Power #4275, a Condor 150 aerial lift bucket truck performs maintenance high above ground at a substation. When fully extended the boom platform can reach a height of 150 feet. #4275 was designed and built by Time Manufacturing Company of Waco, Texas who has been building and assembling aerial lift equipment for the power generation, power distribution and power transmission industries since 1965. The Condor rides on a FWD 8X6 truck carrier chassis. FWD of Clintonville, Wisconsin built America's first all wheel drive vehicle in 1908 and continues today to design and manufacture severe duty all wheel drive trucks and truck chassis.

A 4 drum wire puller is reeling in the ropes that are attached to line cable ends, as it applies tension to the lines. Arizona Public Service truck #22189 is a heavy duty Oshkosh F-2146 series 6X6 truck which has a new style aluminum truck cab that was developed by Oshkosh Truck Corporation of Oshkosh, Wisconsin as a prototype for use in the construction of military vehicles. #22189 was built in 2002 and has a 335hp Cummins ISX diesel, a 5 speed Allison automatic transmission, a two speed transfer case, a 25,000 pound front drive axle and 46,000 pound rear ends. Oshkosh Truck Corporation was founded in 1917 and is recognized the world over as both a leader and an innovator in the manufacture of severe duty specialty transport vehicles.

This Oshkosh 6X6 wire tensioner was originally built for the U.S. Army as an M-911, a 10 ton tank transporter prime mover. Due to the fact that they are designed to operate flawlessly in less than ideal environments and circumstances and because of the excellent maintenance and low operating hours that these vehicles are exposed to, many heavy duty military vehicles find their way home to perform a myriad of civilian duties. Because of its design and construction, this truck is worthy of its namesake and is well suited for its new life as an off road wire puller. The 20,000 pound lift axle has been removed and a special 3 drum winch mechanism body has been installed which will enable this all wheel drive to work in the high voltage power line construction industry for many, many years. The M-911 was delivered with a 430hp Detroit 8V92T-90 diesel engine, a 5 speed Allison automatic transmission, a 2 speed auxiliary transmission, a 26,000 pound front drive axle and 65,000 pound rear ends.

A large Mack 6X6 M-123 truck has a huge single drum wire puller in tow for Irby Construction Company. The trailer is being used to help install a high voltage electric transmission line in some very rough desert surroundings for which the trailer and truck #578 753 have been assembled. With all wheel drive, a 300hp Cummins diesel, a 5 speed transmission with a 2 speed transfer case and 13 inch high clearance, this ex military tank transporter is well suited for its assignment. Irby Construction Company has been in the electric power line construction business since 1917 and today is recognized as a leader in that industry.

An Infrasource Transmission Services International TD25 has just been loaded upon a Fontaine 2+3 heavy haul lowbed trailer. The Fontaine trailer was delivered with a 2 axle jeep which is used when the trailer hauls heavier loads forming a 2+3+2 lowbed trailer. A 3 axle Peterbilt 378 truck tractor has backed under the trailers gooseneck forming an 8 axle truck with trailer heavy haul combination. The TD25 is not just another bulldozer. Besides being able to make access roads in really rough territory, this dozer has been equipped with 3 hydraulic rear winches which are used in the construction of power lines. The winches enable the dozer to help assemble power line transmission towers as well as pull and tension power line cables. Fontaine Trailer Company, founded in 1945, manufacturers heavy haul lowbed trailers in Jasper, Alabama.

Originally built for the United States military by American Hoist and Derrick as a 20 ton 4X4 rough terrain crane, this "Moon Buggy" has lost its upper and found a new life as a high voltage power line pole and equipment transporter. This MDL 2385 was delivered new with a 265hp V-8 Cummins diesel and came with an automatic transmission torque converter drive system that supplies power to the front and rear planetary axles. With its all wheel drive, this crane carrier chassis can operate with 2 wheel or 4 wheel steering and with its low center of gravity it has no problems getting the job done!

High voltage electric power line construction requires specially built heavy duty trucks to transport the equipment and materials needed to construct and install the lines. The rough western geography is no place for unproven equipment and the power line contractors who build these power lines expect their equipment to perform under the roughest of circumstances. S.E. Inc., #700 is a 1964 Kenworth L923 6X6 line truck tractor. Equipped with a Cummins 250hp diesel, a 10 speed transmission and a two speed transfer case, this veteran can tackle the toughest of environments. Companies that use this type of specialized transportation equipment take exceptionally good care of their vehicles and know that they can rely on their equipment when they need it. A metal prefab power pole section is loaded on an expandable pole trailer and is headed up the side of mountainous desert terrain for installation. S.E. Incorporated of Deaver, Wyoming has been constructing western power lines and substations since 1983.

A 2007 Western Star 4900 truck tractor sits while a John Deere "sucker hoe" trans loads the truck's self steering pole trailer with 80 foot long sections of pipe from a rail car. When loaded, the Western Star will transport its load to a pipe stockpile where the pipe will be unloaded and stored until it is needed. This equipment belongs to Pe Ben USA of Houston, Texas who has been in the pipe transportation logistics business since 1957.

CAT
964
MACK
OVERSIZE

A Cat "sucker hoe" is loading an 80 foot long section of 36 inch pipe onto a Dun Transportation and Stringing self steering pole trailer which is being pulled by an R model Mack truck tractor. The "sucker hoe" is a pipe vacuum lift which was specifically designed and developed for the pipe line construction industry. Trucks #946 and #965 are 1986 Mack truck tractors, which are part of a fleet of Bulldogs that are extremely well maintained. Dun Transportation and Stringing Inc. has been hauling pipe line construction materials for over 90 years.

Lowbeds

Specialized transportation trailers that are designed and fabricated to move Oversize equipment and loads. Lowbed trailers can be built with interchangeable components that can allow trailers to be assembled with an assortment of jeeps, dollies and decks that will allow for multiple axle configurations.

This immaculate 1966 Freightliner day cab COE belongs to LaRue Truck Service of Yermo, California. #2 was delivered new to Harrah's Transportation with a single rear axle. After acquiring the classic Freightliner, LaRue Merrifield completely rebuilt it from the frame up. The frame was lengthened to accept a 44,000 pound screw. A Cummins 400 big cam II motor was installed along with a 13 speed transmission.
LaRue also designed, fabricated and built the special 8 tire trailer that he uses to haul railroad cabooses, which became very popular as cabins and guest houses when the railroads ceased using them in the 1980's. A caboose weighs 52,000 pounds without the trucks, which are transported separately on the same trailer. LaRue Merrifield has been in the specialized hauling business for over 50 years.

For over 30 years Maggini and Sons' bright "Triple A" yellow Peterbilts with green flames and high polished chrome and aluminum trim have been delivering hay across the state of California. Their 362 COE (cab over engine) "hay racks" are some of the nicest trucks to travel the San Joaquin Valley and are perennial truck show winners. This sharp Peterbilt 379 heavy haul truck tractor with matching "Triple A" yellow Murray lowbed heavy haul trailer are true California classics. New in 2000, this 379 sports 8 inch chrome stacks, big chrome single headlamps and is equipped with a 550hp Cat C15 diesel and an 18 speed transmission. Maggini & Son Hay Company & Heavy Haul of Riverdale, California operates two dozen of the sharpest Peterbilts to be found anywhere hauling hay and heavy equipment. Their heavy haul lowbed trailers were manufactured in Stockton, California by Harley Murray Inc. who has been building specialized trailers for over 40 years.

This 5 axle heavy haul combination belongs to McCarty Towing of Downey California. Truck #RT8 is a 1994 Freightliner "Classic XL" hooked up to a 16 tire Murray 2 axle trailer. A Hitachi mine shovel bucket is loaded on the Murray "Professional" 16 tire heavy equipment trailer. Power for RT-8 is supplied by a 475hp Cat 3406E diesel which is coupled to an 18 speed transmission. RT-8 has 46,000 pound two speed rear ends.

What at first appears to be a regular "off the shelf" Cat 583 pipe layer is in fact a highly specialized piece of emergency response equipment. This Cat side boom has been specifically designed for use in cleaning up railroad derailments. Weighing in at 82,000 pounds, this 583 can be transported rather quickly to the derailment site where its counter weights and boom, which are transported on another truck, can be re-attached quite quickly. The 583 remains loaded on its lowbed trailer at all times and is ready to roll on a moment's notice. Emergency response service companies like Hulcher make arrangements with the Department of Transportation (DOT) of various states that allow them to move with a pre-arranged oversize transportation permit. This 1998 Peterbilt 378 belongs to Hulcher Emergency Services. With 50 divisions in the United States, Canada and Mexico, they are the largest operator of railroad re-rail equipment in North America. The Pete's 425hp Cat 3406E coupled to a 10 speed transmission has plenty of power to expedite the Cat to its next job site.

Wearing a very attractive purple flames over white paint scheme is Silver State Trucking #120. Hooked up to the big 1996 Kenworth T800W is a 16 tire Peerless jeep and a 16 tire 60 ton Trailmobile trailer. A brand new Komatsu PC1800 crawler shovel frame with body has been loaded upon the heavy duty Trailmobile 16 tire trailer. Under the hood of Silver State #120 is a powerful 550hp Cat 3406E motor that has been mated to an 18 speed transmission. Supplying the traction for #120 are dual speed 46,000 pound rear ends. The Peerless jeep was manufactured in Portland, Oregon while the Trailmobile trailer was made in Berkley, California.

A 125,000 pound Cat D9 with slope board has been loaded upon CMI Transportation's Murray Load Master trailer. Although this is a 7 axle heavy haul combination, its legally permitted haul capacity is 60 tons due to the 16 tire jeep and 16 tire trailer. Pulling this load is a very attractive 1999 Peterbilt 378 heavy haul truck tractor whose drive train components include a 500hp Cat C15 diesel, an 18 speed transmission and dual speed 46,000 pound rear ends. CMI Transportation is located in Lake Elsinore, California and has been hauling heavy over sized loads for nearly 20 years.

Triple R Heavy Haul #3 is a 1989 Peterbilt 379 that has been loaded with a 105,000 pound Caterpillar 634 scraper. The scraper's front end is chained down to a Cozad 16 tire jeep while its rear end is suspended on a Cozad 8 tire stinger dolly. This scraper transport combination is another variation of the 16 tire scraper basket with 16 tire jeep concept. Truck #3 has a Cat 3408 air to air motor that delivers 650hp to a mated 5X4 gear box. The dual speed 48,000 lb rear ends are from Eaton. Triple R Heavy Haul calls Stockton, California home and has been in the specialized transportation business since 1977.

Dalton Trucking #111 is a Peterbilt 378 pulling a Murray 16 tire jeep with a Murray 16 tire scraper basket that also has a Murray 4 tire weight booster attached to it to help distribute the weight of its load, a 116,000 pound Cat water pull. Power for #111 comes from a Cummins 500hp diesel that drives 46,000 pound dual speed rear ends through an 18 speed transmission. Dalton Trucking's home offices and shops are located in Fontana, California and their trucks have been a familiar sight on Southern California roadways since 1963.

This brand new Freightliner "Classic XL" belongs to the University of Texas. Sitting on the truck's 3 axle Talbert heavy haul lowbed trailer is a seismic "Thumper". The seismic thumper is a vehicle that is used to create a series of seismic waves by thumping the ground with the big plate that is attached to the bottom of the vehicles frame. The seismic vibrations are then recorded by the thumper to see if the ground might hold petroleum deposits below. New in 2007, this Freightliner FLD 120 SD was delivered with a 525hp Detroit Diesel series 60 motor, an 18 speed transmission and dual speed 46,000 pound rear ends. The 3 axle lowbed heavy haul trailer was manufactured by Talbert Manufacturing Inc. of Rennselaer, Indiana who has been building specialized transportation trailers since 1938.

A 67,000 pound track alignment machine is loaded on a Load King "Power Fold" automatic folding gooseneck trailer. The trailer's folding gooseneck allows the trailer to be loaded and unloaded from the rails. Load King has installed loading rails in both the trailer deck and the gooseneck deck at their manufacturing facility located at Elk Point, South Dakota. Union Pacific #1915-60915 is a 2000 Kenworth W900B. A 475hp Cat 3406E motor provides power to the 46,000 pound rear ends through an 18 speed transmission.

An AGM A40LN articulated off road water truck manufactured by American Global Manufacturing rides on an XL Specialized Trailers 4 axle heavy haul lowbed trailer. A Western Star 4964 4 axle heavy haul truck tractor pulls this impressive 8 axle combination. The A40LN was fabricated and assembled by AGM at their Tempe, Arizona facility. The heavy haul lowbed trailer was fabricated and assembled in Manchester, Iowa by XL who has been building specialized trailers for agricultural, construction and heavy haul customers since 1995.

Paul DeLong Heavy Haul #800 is a "Legacy Class Edition" series Peterbilt 379. Peterbilt produced over 230,000 model 379's from 1986 until April 2007 when the new Peterbilt Model 389 went into production. Starting in August of 2006 the final run of the Model 379 was a special commemorative edition that was limited to just a 1000 units.

Paul Delong #800 was built in 2007 and wears Legacy Class Edition builders plate number #767. Painted a hot "Viper Red", this exquisite heavy haul truck tractor was delivered from the factory with a 550hp Cat C15 diesel motor, an 18 speed transmission and dual speed 46,000 pound rear ends. A 156,000 pound Liebherr rock truck frame assembly has been loaded upon Paul Delong's Rackley 9 axle trailer for delivery to Houston, Texas. Rackley Trailers are designed and assembled in Stockton, California. "Rackley bilt" trailers feature oval shaped frame rail "cut outs".

Paul Delong Heavy Haul is based out of Las Vegas, Nevada and has been in the specialized transportation business since 1976. His bright red Peterbilts are a familiar sight hauling heavy oversize loads throughout the Western United States.

Reeve Trucking Company of Stockton, California was founded in 1976. Their commitment to hard work, safety and customer service has made them one of the largest specialized cargo carriers in the state of California and the Southwest. Reeve Trucking primarily serves the construction industry and they are the largest haulers of bridge girders, concrete products, prestressed piling and structural steel in California.

Reeve Trucking operates a fleet of 100 company owned trucks of which 20 are dedicated to the specialized heavy haul customer. They take great pride in the appearance of their equipment and this 9 axle truck with trailer is an example of that pride.

Pulling the Cozad 2+2+2 trailer is a bright green Freightliner FLD 120 SD which was assembled in Portland Oregon in 2001. L7 has a 600hp Cummins ISX diesel, 18 speed transmission and 46,000 pound rear ends. A 92,000 pound Liebherr LR1280 crane "upper" sits on the trailer's deck.

Tatel Heavy Haul Trucking #86 loads a Wabco 120 rock truck chassis on its blue Cozad 2+2+2 lowbed heavy haul trailer. This Kenworth T800 wears an attractive blue and white paint scheme. Truck #86 was delivered new in 1993. Drive train components feature a 460hp Cat 3406B diesel motor, an 18 speed transmission and dual speed 46,000 pound rear ends.

Kenworth #9721, a W900L model, wears the classic red over white paint scheme of Sherman Brothers Heavy Trucking out of Harrisburg, Oregon. Family owned and operated since 1969, they can be found operating in 11 Western States and Canada. #9721 has a 550hp Cat power plant, 18 speed transmission and dual speed rear ends. An 89,000 pound Grove RT-760E rough terrain crane is being transported on the 2+2+2 heavy haul trailer from General Trailer. Since 1953, General Trailer has been manufacturing trailers in Springfield, Oregon and they are very popular with the logging and construction industries of the Pacific Northwest.

Elite Specialized Transport #108 is a 2007 Kenworth T800H heavy haul tractor. Sitting under the hood of this handsome rig is a 625hp C15 Cat power plant. Truck #108 came from the factory with an 18 speed transmission which is couple to 46,000 pound dual speed rear ends. Loaded on the deck of the 2+2+2 trailer is a Haulmax 3770D rock truck that was manufactured in Australia. The circular frame rail “cut outs” identify this as a Cozad trailer which was manufactured in Stockton, California.

This sharp white 2000 Peterbilt 379 heavy haul truck tractor belongs to B&B Inc. of Havre, Montana. A 135,000 pound Cat 777 rock truck has been loaded on to a 2+2+2 Siebert lowbed heavy haul trailer. B&B #1 has a Cat 3406E diesel, an 18 speed transmission and dual speed 46,000 pound rear ends. Siebert Trailers were manufactured in Stockton, California from the mid 1970's until 1991 when they were acquired by Kalyn Manufacturing Co. Inc. of Gatesville, Texas forming the Kalyn Siebert Trailer Division.

Since it was founded in 1967, Midwest Specialized Transportation of Rochester, Minnesota has been dedicated to meeting the many needs of its customers. As a result of their dedication to customer service and their commitment to safety, Midwest has been recognized as one of the best specialized transportation firms in the industry. Midwest serves the continental United States and Canada.

Truck #385 is a 1999 International Eagle. This clean heavy haul tractor is pulling a brand new Trail King 2+2+2 with a 120,000 pound Terex RT100 Rough Terrain Crane. Truck #385 was delivered with a 550hp Cat 3406E diesel motor, an 18 speed transmission and dual speed 46,000 pound rear ends.

Loaded on the deck of a Sierra Rental & Transport Murray 2+2+2 M2000 trailer is a 135,000 pound Cat 777B rock truck. Hooked up to this impressive load is SRT #167, a 2006 Peterbilt 357. Power to move the Cat 777B will come from the Pete's 550hp Cummins ISX diesel motor, which will provide traction to the 46,000 pound dual speed rear ends through an 18 speed transmission. Sierra Rental & Transport of Sparks, Nevada offers its customers over 37 years of lowbed heavy haul experience.

This impressive Western Star 4964SX heavy haul truck tractor belongs to SSK Transportation of Irving, Texas. Delivered new in 1999, #30 has a powerful drive train that consists of a 475hp Cat 3406E motor, an 18 speed transmission with dual speed 52,000 pound rear ends. A 105,000 pound Cat scraper rides on a Kalyn Siebert 2+2+2 low bed heavy haul trailer. A 9 axle heavy haul combination is formed when this trailer is hooked up to the big Western Star. The Kalyn Siebert lowbed heavy haul trailer was manufactured at their Gatesville, Texas facility, which has been building heavy specialized trailers since the mid 1970's.

The classic charcoal grey Peterbilt with high polished aluminum trim of Bill Sign's Trucking have been turning heads throughout southern California and the Western United States since 1984. These awesome trucks have set a standard that even today is still followed by the industry. Sitting on an Aspen 2+2+2 lowbed trailer is a 90,000 pound Cat water pull. The 2000 Peterbilt 378 heavy haul tractor has a 600hp Cat C16 power plant, an 18 speed transmission and dual speed 46,000 pound rear ends. The matching green heavy haul lowbed trailer was manufactured by Aspen Custom Trailers of Leduc, Alberta, Canada. Aspen has been designing, fabricating and assembling specialized transportation trailers since the 1980's.

This sharp 10 axle heavy haul combination is leased to Specialized Transport Service of San Antonio, Texas. Truck #109 is a 4 axle 2002 Peterbilt 379 heavy haul truck tractor which has a 600hp Cat C16 diesel, an 18 speed main transmission, a 2 speed auxiliary transmission and dual speed 46,000 pound rear ends. A 135,000 pound Cat 777B rock truck rides on the beam rails of a Cozad 2+2+2 heavy haul lowbed trailer, which was manufactured in Stockton, California. For nearly 50 years Cozad Trailers has been designing and building custom specialized lowbed trailers for the heavy haul transportation industry.

Energy Transportation Inc., of Casper Wyoming, operates more than 65 heavy haul tractors throughout the West. Their commitment to operating and maintaining the best equipment available is evidenced by truck #148, a pristine white 2003 Peterbilt 379 heavy haul tractor, pulling a 3+3+2 Trail King trailer. The tractor has a 550hp Caterpillar C15 diesel, an 18 speed transmission and 52,000 pound Eaton rear axles. Sitting on the Trail King deck is a P&H shovel bucket headed for a mine in Northern Nevada. The Trail King trailer was manufactured in Mitchell, South Dakota and the triangular "cut outs" in the trailer frame side rails are unique to Trail King trailers. Trail King Industries has been manufacturing heavy haul trailers since 1983. Energy Transportation, Inc. has been furnishing first class service to the construction, mining, petroleum and energy development industries of the Rocky Mountain West since 1985.

A 120,000 pound refractor, bound for a mine in Baton Rouge, Louisiana, rides on a Cozad 3+3+3 heavy haul lowbed trailer with a 53 foot deck. Pulling this Oversize Load is IOSTY Trucking #1, a beautiful blue and black 2007 Kenworth T800W. The Kenworth was delivered from the factory with a 550hp Cat C15 power plant and has an 18 speed transmission with a 52,000 pound dual speed rear end. The total length of the combination, from the truck's front bumper to the rear of the trailer, is 152 feet.

Sparkling in the late afternoon sun is this absolutely flawless 13 axle heavy haul rig operated by Palletized Trucking of Houston, Texas. Truck #915 pulls a 142,000 pound LeTourneau L-1150 wheel loader rear frame assembly on its custom built 3+3+3 Kalyn Siebert lowbed heavy haul trailer. #915 is a 2007 Peterbilt 379 which was delivered from the factory with a 565hp Cummins ISX diesel, an 18 speed transmission and dual speed rear ends. The total length of this rig, from front bumper to rear bumper is 146 feet. The total gross weight of this rig is 245,000 pounds. Palletized Trucking has been operating from its Houston, Texas terminals since 1969. Kalyn Siebert has been designing and building specialized transportation trailers since the mid 1970's. This awesome trailer with its square hole "cut outs" in its frame rails was designed, fabricated and built in their modern shop facility located in Gatesville, Texas.

This awesome 13 axle heavy haul combination belongs to Ken Galyean Trucking of Draper, Utah. Power for this immaculate 27 year old Kenworth W900 comes from a Cat 3406E that supplies 460hp to a 15 speed main gear box that is coupled to a 4 speed Spicer auxiliary. The 2 speed rear ends are rated at 46,000 pounds. The 3+3+3 Cozad beam trailer has been extensively modified by the owner to suit his specific needs. A 150,000 pound Cat 797 rock truck frame is being loaded for a trip to the coal mines near Gillette, Wyoming.

Two underground mine excavators sit on a Trail King 3+3+3 lowboy trailer owned by Lucia Specialized Hauling of Schenectady, New York. At the head end of the Trail King trailer is #1007, a 1994 Western Star "Heritage" 4964F four axle heavy truck tractor. #1007 was delivered new to Lucia with a 475hp Cat 3406E motor, a Fuller 18 speed transmission and 46,000 pound dual speed Eaton rear ends. A 25,000 pound lift axle sits behind the cab. Lucia Specialized Hauling has been providing transportation solutions to customers in the Eastern United States for over 25 years.

Pulling an all black Liddell 3+3+3 lowbed heavy haul trailer is Badger Transport truck #87, a sharp 2007 4 axle Peterbilt 379 heavy haul tractor. When both the truck and trailer are hooked up together they form a 13 axle heavy haul combination. Truck #87 is equipped with a 625hp Cat diesel and an 18 speed transmission. Badger Transport Inc. of Clintonville, Wisconsin has been in the specialized transport business for over 25 years. The impressive Liddell lowbed trailer was manufactured in Springville, Alabama.

Super Tankers

Tank train bodies and trailers are constructed of aluminum, fiber glass and steel and can be lined and insulated. They can haul crude petroleum products, fuels, food grade products, liquid asphalt, milk, slurry, water and even wine.

Reflecting a very clean corporate image is this Chevron Corporation fuel delivery tank truck with trailer. #704 is a 2007 Peterbilt 385 that is equipped with a Cat C series diesel and a 13 speed transmission. #704 is making a delivery at the Nevada state line and has a matching set of Heil fuel tank bodies which can carry 4800 gallons up front, with an additional 7000 gallons in the trailer.

In Nevada the maximum GVW, gross vehicle weight, for this truck with trailer combination is 129,000 pounds. #704 is 500 feet away from the California state line where #704's weight and length would be illegal because California DOT regulations only allow for a GVW of 80,000 pounds.

For over 33 years KB Oil has been supplying fuel and bulk petroleum products to customers in southeastern Nevada and southwestern Utah. KB Oil is family owned and takes a great deal of pride in their business as is evidenced by the appearance of their convenience stores and their fleet of 24 delivery trucks. It is hard to believe that truck #506 is 9 years old. This pristine Kenworth W900L was delivered new in 2000. All of KB Oil's Kenworth's have big Cat power plants as does #506. A 600hp Cat C16 sits under the hood while an 18 speed transmission helps to move the big KW with matching polished aluminum Beall tank bodies effortlessly down the road.

Flying J Inc. operates nearly 260 Travel Plazas and fuel stops in North America and Canada. They maintain a modern fleet of more than 600 delivery trucks which help them to deliver over 11 million gallons of petroleum products each day. Wearing the very colorful Fly J paint scheme and helping to deliver over 1200 loads a day is truck #873, a brand new Navistar 9400i which is equipped with a 475hp Cummins ISX motor and a 10 speed transmission. #873 is pulling a matched set of Beall Trans Liner "Rocky Mountain" double aluminum fuel trailers.

This impressive twin steer Western Star 4900SA super tanker belongs to Rebel Oil Co. New in 2004, #252 was delivered with two 20,000 pound front axles, a 515hp Detroit series 60 power plant and a 10 speed transmission. The matching polished aluminum Beall fuel tanks can hold a combined maximum legal load capacity of over 13,000 gallons. Rebel Oil operates over 50 convenience store fuel stations and their immaculate white delivery trucks can be found in Nevada and Arizona making deliveries to their stores and their many customers. Rebel Oil has been business for over 57 years.

Sporting a very classy red paint scheme is Jenkin's Oil #35, a 2005 Peterbilt 379. The drive train for #35 includes a 550 hp Cat C15 with a 13 speed transmission. The super tanker's main tank was built by Trailmobile while the pup was made by Beall. Jenkins Oil operates a fleet of 18 super tankers and has been delivering fuel to their many customers since 1976.

With a matching set of Beall Trans Liner tank trailers in tow, CLX Trucking #B08 is in route to pick up 13,500 gallons of diesel fuel. This 1994 Peterbilt 379 is equipped with a 500hp Cat 3406E diesel and an 18 speed transmission that help this bulk fuel Super Tanker to complete its 500 mile long round trip from Ely, Nevada to North Las Vegas and return.

The Keenan Advantage Group is the nation's largest bulk transporter of refined petroleum products. Nationally KAG operates 100 terminals and 98 satellite locations which enable them to operate in 38 states and serve the 48 continental United States and Canada. Besides petroleum products, KAG is also one of the nation's largest bulk transporters of chemicals and bulk liquid food products. This Freightliner Columbia tank truck with trailer wears the attractive new KAG paint scheme. It has a 400hp Mercedes diesel motor, a 10 speed transmission and it is outfitted with matching Heil fuel tanks.

This immaculate Kenworth W900L hauls milk for the Great Basin Dairy Group of Delta, Utah. New in 2008, truck #19 has a 550hp Cat C15 diesel and an 18 speed transmission. The matching set of stainless steel dairy tank trailers were manufactured by Beall Trailers of Billings, Montana.

A Ruan Transportation Management Systems Inc. "milk train" consisting of a matched set of West-Mark milk tank trailers sits behind a Freightliner Columbia lettered for Jim Aartman Inc. of Ripon California. Jim Aartman was founded in California in 1967 and was a nationwide bulk food grade carrier that was acquired by Ruan in 2007.

Truck #490 is equipped with a 475hp Cat C15 diesel and a 10 speed transmission. The milk tank trailers were manufactured in Atwater, California by West-Mark Tank Trailers who has been manufacturing food grade tank trailers for over 40 years. West-Mark also manufactures fire apparatus. Ruan Transportation Management Systems is one of the nation's largest bulk transportation carriers. Ruan started hauling gravel in Iowa in 1932.

Pulling a compressed gas tanker train for BOC GASSES is #169, a 2000 Kenworth T800B. The main tank carries 65,000 pounds while the rear tank carries 22,000 pounds. A Cat C13 series diesel engine provides 435hp and it is coupled to an 18 speed transmission that helps to move this smart looking tank train from Utah to Wyoming and Nevada. The trailers were manufactured in Lubbock, Texas by Lubbock Trailers Inc.

When this Aggregate Industries Peterbilt isn't pulling a matched set of bottom dump trailers it is used to haul hot asphalt and hot oil from a distribution center to the asphalt batch plant. To pull a maximum GVW, gross vehicle weight, of 129.000 pounds the Peterbilt 378 has been equipped with a 425hp Cat 3406E diesel and an 18 speed transmission. The asphalt train consists of two Beall insulated aluminum trailers that were designed especially for this type of liquid bulk materials transport. Aggregate Industries US operates six regional building materials divisions that service 16 states. They manufacture and supply a broad range of aggregate based building materials. Aggregate Industries corporate office is located in Rockville, Maryland.

NU Equipment truck #2010 has just unloaded two tanks of hot liquid asphalt from its matching set of insulated aluminum Beall tank trailers at an asphalt batch plant in St. George, Utah. #2010 is a 1999 Kenworth W900L which has a 475hp Cat 3406E diesel, a 13 speed transmission and 46,000 pound rear ends. Besides hauling oil, emulsion and water, NU Equipment, of North Las Vegas, Nevada also hauls aggregates, asphalt, fill materials and debris as well as heavy construction equipment.

Powder Trains

Powder trains haul dry bulk products in pneumatic covered hoppers. These "air slides" can haul aggregates, carbonite, cement, cinders, crushed coal, fertilizer, fly ash, gypsum, lime, pellets, silica, and soda ash. They can also haul wet loads such as slurry.

Hartwick and Hand truck #63 pulls a matched set of 3 J&L Tank pneumatic covered hoppers. The triple air slide trailers are loaded with silica sand which will be used to make glass. Hartwick & Hand Inc. has been providing California and Nevada with bulk commodity transportation services from their Victorville, California terminal since 1961. Supplying power for this powder train is truck #63, a 1996 Freightliner FLD which has a 350hp Cat diesel and a 10 speed transmission. J&L Tank is a division of Heil Trailers International of Athens, Georgia.

CTI Inc. truck #459, a Kenworth W900B, pulls a powder train that consists of a matched set of triple J&L Tank pneumatic covered hoppers. Using Kenworth and Peterbilt truck tractors equipped with 350hp diesel motors, 10 speed transmissions and 40,000 pound rear ends, Cement Transporters Inc. hauls primarily dry bulk products with their bright red trucks that have been a familiar sight throughout the great southwest for nearly 40 years. Founded with one truck in 1930 as a local freight carrier in Tucson, Arizona, this family owned company today operates a fleet of 400 truck tractors and is the largest cement hauler in Arizona. CTI Inc. serves Arizona, New Mexico, Texas and California from 12 terminals and they also operate flatbed trailers and live bottom dump trailers to handle the needs of their many customers.

Barney Trucking #203 drops a load of crushed coal into an auger from its matched set of 175 cubic feet Beall covered pneumatic hopper trailers. The auger is located beneath a rail car "shaker" on a coal unloading track. Truck #203 is a 1999 Peterbilt 378 which is equipped with a 475hp Cat C15 diesel, a 10 speed transmission and 44,000 pound rear ends. Starting with 1 truck in 1947 Barney Trucking now operates more than 275 trucks and serves industrial, mining, energy and construction industries throughout the West. Family owned, Barney Trucking transports and delivers dry bulk products to customers in Utah, Nevada, California, Arizona, New Mexico, Wyoming, Idaho and Montana from their 3 terminals in Utah and Nevada.

Pulling a matched set of J&L covered pneumatic hoppers is Nelson's Sunbeam Coal truck #N17, a 1999 Kenworth W900L. Truck #N17 was delivered with a 550hp Cat C15 diesel, an 18 speed transmission and dual speed rear ends. This powder train is loading lime for the return trip home to Salina, Utah, where Nelson's Sunbeam Coal operates a coal and coke loading facility. The pneumatic "air slides" were manufactured by Heil Trailer International of Athens, Georgia at their Rhome, Texas assembly plant.

A brand new Peterbilt 389 pulls a set of "B Train" Beall pneumatic covered hoppers. The trailers are joined together without the use of a rear dolly by a fifth wheel. The fifth wheel is located over the last axle on the lead trailer. This Powder Train is operated by Dick Irvin Incorporated of Shelby, Montana. The sharp looking Pete has a 550hp Cummins ISX diesel, an 18 speed transmission and dual speed 46,000 pound rear ends.

Having just loaded it's matched set of Beall pneumatic covered hoppers with silica sand, a Savage Companies powder train prepares to weigh its total gross vehicle weight and start its delivery journey. Pulling the train is truck S1252, a 2003 Mack CL733 which was delivered new with a 500hp Cummins ISX diesel, an 8LL transmission and 40,000 pound dual speed rear ends. The Savage Companies were founded in 1946 by the Savage Brothers who started hauling building materials from American Fork, Utah. Today, the Savage Companies deliver bulk cargo products throughout the United States and Canada and they offer their customers bulk transportation services that include truck, rail and marine delivery.

Carbonite from a mine in Southern California's Lucerne Valley fills both 775 cubic foot Beall pneumatic covered hoppers belonging to D.P. Curtis Trucking of Richfield, Utah. This "Powder Train" is not legal in California so the driver must drop a trailer at the California state line at Primm, Nevada and continue on into California to pick up the first load. After dropping the first loaded trailer back at state line, he will repeat the trip and the load out with the second trailer and then return again to state line where he will reassemble his powder train so that he can now legally return to his delivery destination in Utah.

D.P. Curtis operates a fleet of over 55 modern truck tractors, an example is truck #248 a 2006 Western Star which has been equipped with a 475hp Cat C15 motor and an 18 speed transmission, which will help to get the matched set of polished aluminum Beall "air slides" to their destination. D.P. Curtis Trucking has been in business since 1982 primarily serving Southwestern Utah, Northern Arizona and Southern Nevada but they also operate throughout the continental United States. Along with their fleet of "air slides", D.P. Curtis also operates bottom dumps and flatbeds.

Chance Corporation operates a modern fleet of bulk transportation equipment from their terminals located in Window Rock and Fredonia, Arizona. Their fleet includes Peterbilt 378 truck tractors that are equipped with 525hp Cat C15 diesel motors and 13 speed transmissions. Truck #C104 pulls a powder train that consists of a matched set of J&L Tank pneumatic covered hoppers which were manufactured in Rhome, Texas by Heil Trailer International who acquired J&L Tank in 1993. Chance Corporation has been in business since 1971.

A brand new matched set of polished aluminum Beall pneumatic trailers shine in the afternoon sun. These trailers were manufactured at Beall Corporation's Billings, Montana facility and were delivered to Ready Mix Inc. to service their Las Vegas area batch plants. Power to pull this powder train will come from truck #5051, a brand new Kenworth W900B truck tractor that is equipped with a 475hp Cat C15 diesel, a 10 speed transmission and 46,000 pound rear ends. Ready Mix Inc. was founded in 1996 and operates cement batch plants in Arizona and Nevada.

This powder train belongs to Buffalo Building Materials of Las Vegas, Nevada. Pulling a matched set of Beall aluminum covered pneumatic hoppers is truck #14, a 2006 Kenworth T800. Truck #14 has been equipped with a 535hp Cummins ISX diesel, a 10 speed transmission and 46,000 pound rear ends which enable this powerful KW to pull its maximum 129,000 pound gross vehicle weight with ease.

Dumps, Hoppers and Tubs

Road Trains that transport mostly aggregates, asphalt, cinders, coal, debris, earth, fill, gravel, gypsum and sand using bottom dump trailers, end dump trailers, side dump trailers and transfer tub sets.

Three sets of these "Super Double" bottom dumps operated on a private haul road moving sand and aggregate from a pit to a Nevada Ready Mix cement batch plant. These massive "Monsters of the Midway" were manufactured by M-R-S, Mississippi Road Service, of Flora, Mississippi. All three 4 wheel tractors have 600hp Cummins KTA power plants with Allison automatic transmissions. The trailers were manufactured by Challenge-Cook Brothers Corporation of Los Angeles, California and their total capacity was "guesstimated" to be over 75 cubic yards for each trailer, over 100 tons. Today, MRS Tractors are custom built to order by Taylor Machine Works, Inc.

A set of SmithCo side dump trailers owned by Diamond Construction Company unloads its dirt train as another set of side dumps waits for its turn to unload. SmithCo Maufacturing of LeMars, Iowa has been building trailers since 1993 and today, they offer several different models of side dump trailers for the construction industry. This Peterbilt 378 is equipped with a 475hp Cat diesel and an 18 speed transmission.

The long handsome hood of a Peterbilt 379 is unmistakable. Neal Trucking Inc. of Riverside, California operates two of these sharp two tone blue triple transfer sets which are used to haul cinders from a mine near Lathrop Wells, Nevada to cinder block plants located in Las Vegas. Both of these 2001 Petes are equipped with 525hp Cat C15 diesels and 13 speed transmissions. The matching triple transfer sets were manufactured by Rogue Truck Body LLC, of Kirby, Oregon. Since 1990, Rogue has been building custom dump bodies to meet the specific demands and requirements of each individual customer. Neal Trucking has been in the construction materials transport business since 1976 and has 70 trucks dedicated to meeting the various needs of their customers which includes hauling dry bulk, aggregate and flatbed loads.

An immaculate 1980 Peterbilt 359 pulls a matched set of triple SmithCo model S1 side dump trailers. The classic 359 belongs to Marc Williams of Las Vegas, Nevada whose family has been in the construction business for over 30 years. The Pete has a 450hp Cat 3408 V8 diesel, a 15 speed transmission and 48,000 pound rear ends. The trailers were manufactured in LeMars, Iowa by SmithCo Trailers who has been building side dump trailers for the construction industry since 1993.

A pair of single axle Peterbilt 378's each pull matched sets of 3 Fruehauf 11 yard bottom dump trailers for Wells Cargo Construction Company. Family owned and operated, Wells Cargo was founded in 1935 and is the oldest operating construction company in the state of Nevada. These well maintained 1999 Petes each have 400hp Cummins diesels with 13 speed transmissions. The bottom dump trailers were manufactured in Indianapolis, Indiana by Fruehauf Trailer Company who at one time was North America's largest trailer manufacturer. Fruehauf Trailer Company was founded in Detroit, Michigan in 1918 by August Fruehauf who built the nation's first "semi trailer" which was a boat trailer to be hauled behind a Model T Ford. Fruehauf was acquired by Wabash National Corporation in 1997.

An Autocar AT64 dump truck pulls two 11 cubic yard bottom dump trailers for Southern Nevada Paving Inc. The big Autocar truck was designed to compete with Kenworth and Peterbilt for the west coast owner operator segment of the truck market and was arguably the most handsome truck that Autocar ever built. The bottom dump trailers were manufactured by ACE, American Carrier Equipment Inc. of Fresno, California who has been manufacturing heavy highway construction equipment for over 50 years. SNP has been in business for over 40 years and today is part of Aggregate Industries Inc.

Kuck Trucking Inc. of Big Fork, Montana operates this set of "Rocky Mountain" double bottom dumps. The lead bottom dump trailer is 43 foot long and was manufactured by Load King. The rear pup is 20 foot long and was manufactured by ACE. The Kenworth truck tractor is a 2000 T800 which is equipped with a 460hp Cummins N14 diesel, a 15 speed transmission and 46,000 pound rear ends. Load King Trailers are manufactured in Elk River, South Dakota. Load King is a division of CMI of Oklahoma City, Oklahoma. ACE bottom dump trailers are manufactured by American Carrier Equipment Inc. of Fresno, California.

Sandia Sand, Gravel and Asphalt truck #207 pulls its matched set of Ranco Trailer bottom dumps over an AshRoss 1260C mobile unloading system for belly dump trailers. The Rancos will drop their load into the paving grizzly's hopper which will trans load 40 cubic yards of asphalt into waiting end dump trucks which will then transport the asphalt to its final paving destination. Truck #207 is a Kenworth W900B truck tractor which is equipped with a 425hp Cat 3406E diesel and an 18 speed transmission. The bottom dump trailers were manufactured in Lamar, Colorado by Ranco Trailers who has been building custom designed trailers to meet the needs of agricultural and construction industry customers since 1968.

Las Vegas Paving Corporation operates 30 sets of Red River bottom dump trailers. Depending on the load, these bottom dump trains can legally haul up to 42 tons. Power for the Red River trains is supplied by Peterbilt 378 truck tractors that are equipped with 425hp Cat 3406E diesels with 18 speed transmissions. The trailers were manufactured by Red River Manufacturing of West Fargo, North Dakota, which today is part of Trail King Industries. Las Vegas Paving Corporation was founded in 1958 and is one of the largest excavating, grading and paving contractors in the West.

Rinker Materials Corporation truck #109 is a Peterbilt 378 which pulls a matched set of aluminum bottom dump trailers that were manufactured by Travis Trailers of Houston, Texas. Travis Trailers has been building light weight aluminum dump trailers for the construction industry since 1989. The trailers both have a 24 cubic yard capacity. Rinker Materials Corporation is one of the top 10 heavy building material producers in the world and was acquired by Cemex in 2007.

Silver Bullets

Silver Bullets are only manufactured by Beall Trailer Corporation at their Sunnyside, Washington facility. They are recognized as the finest aluminum bottom dump trailers built. Silver bullets are constructed of aluminum which allows for a greater payload and they are designed and built to stand up under the severest of operating conditions and most rigorous of operating schedules. Silver Bullets can haul aggregates, cinders, coal, earth, fertilizer, gravel, gypsum, pellets and sand. They can be assembled as Rocky Mountain Doubles or Nevada Doubles.

Since 1947 the Robinson family of Salina, Utah has been hauling coal. Today, they haul over 3.5 million tons of coal annually with a modern fleet that consists of over 75 Beall polished aluminum Rocky Mountain double "Silver Bullet" trailer sets. These light weight, high strength trailers were actually conceived and designed by company founder Art Robinson and Beall engineers in 1978 to stand up to the harsh, rigorous demands that were required to meet the grueling nonstop delivery schedule of "coal fired" electric power plants in Utah and Colorado as well as the giant Kennecott Copper mine and facility located at Smelter, Utah near Salt Lake City. Robinson's Silver Bullets are pulled by a fleet that today, consists of modern mostly Kenworth W900B truck tractors that are equipped with 475hp Cat C15 motors, 10 speed transmissions and 46,000 pound rear ends. These trucks pull a 34 cubic yard lead 3 axle trailer coupled to a 32 yard 2 axle rear trailer and when fully loaded they haul 43 tons of coal. The GVW for these coal trains is 129,000 pounds and Robinson operates these units 22 hours a day 5 and sometimes 6 days a week nonstop year round. Beall Trailers are designed, fabricated and assembled in Sunnyside, Washington. Beall Trailers have been building heavy duty lightweight trailers since 1905 and today, they manufacture some of the finest trailers built from their 5 modern facilities located in the Western United States.

Robinson #6 is the only Peterbilt in the fleet. Purchased in 1974, this spectacular Peterbilt 359 was acquired specifically for use as a wrecker by Art Robinson. #6 is powered by a 400hp big cam Cummins diesel which is paired to a 13 speed transmission. A Holmes 750 twin boom wrecker was installed to "take care of business".

Sporting an attractive white with yellow over gray paint scheme and pulling a bright set of polished aluminum Beall "Silver Bullets" is Sierra Ready Mix truck #H03. Sierra Ready Mix has been supplying ready mix concrete products to Las Vegas, Nevada customers since 1994. They operate a modern fleet of Kenworths which includes truck #H03, a 2004 Kenworth W900B which is equipped with a 475hp Cat C15 diesel and a 10 speed transmission. The "Silver Bullets" were manufactured at Beall Corpration's Sunnyside, Washington facility.

Nevada Ready Mix Corporation is Nevada's largest supplier of quality ready mix cement products. NRM operates a fleet of over 250 trucks including truck C10 which is part of a modern well maintained "rubber tired conveyor system" that helps NRM to service the needs of their customers by delivering sand and aggregate to their many batch plants throughout Clark County. Truck C10 is a 1996 Peterbilt 378 which is equipped with a 425hp Cat 3406E diesel, an 18 speed transmission and 46,000 pound rear ends. C10 is one of a group of 27 aggregate trains that consist of Peterbilt 378's that all pull matched sets of Beall Trailer's "Silver Bullets" whose lightweight aluminum construction allows for greater payloads.

Pulling a matched set of aluminum "Silver Bullets" is CSR truck T11, a Peterbilt 378 truck tractor specifically designed and built by Peterbilt to serve the grueling demands of the construction industry. Having been stopped for a "hospitality call" by one of Nevada's finest, truck T11 still wears the blue paint scheme of WMK Materials which was bought out by Colonial Sugar Refineries of Australia in 1990 but it will soon wear a coat of fresh CSR red.

Peterbilt introduced new models in 2006 that would replace their 379 and 378 traditional model conventional trucks. Both the 389 and the 388 wear the new cast aluminum halogen reflector head lamps that are characteristic of these new models. Wearing the new aluminum headlamps is Cemex truck #T118 a Peterbilt 388. The drive train for T118 was spec'd to pull it's matched set of Beall "Silver Bullets" and it includes a 525hp Cummins ISX diesel, an 18 speed transmission and 46,000 pound rear ends. Cemex was founded in Mexico in 1906 and today is North America's largest producer of cement and cement products.

Super Flats

Flatbed trailer Road Trains that haul agricultural products, building materials, cement and concrete products, equipment, forest products and wall board. The maximum length for these trains in Nevada and Utah is 115 feet from king pin to end of train.

Sitting behind an immaculate 1986 Peterbilt 359 are three matching Utility flat bed trailers loaded with fresh horse hay from the lush fields of northern Nevada. A set of modern rectangular head lamps from a newer 379 model Peterbilt has been added to the classic 24 year old 359 whose drive train includes a 425hp Cat 3406B engine, an 18 speed transmission and 46,000 pound rear ends. It is quite apparent that the owner operator of this truck takes a great deal of pride in his business and his truck. Utility Trailer Manufacturing Company has been building trailers since 1914.

This classic Peterbilt 362 COE belongs to Carey Transport of Fallon, Nevada. New in 2001, #59 is equipped with a 475hp Cat C15 and a 13 speed transmission. An evenly spaced load of wall board has been loaded upon the rigs matching Utility trailers. Carey operates a fleet of 362's and has been delivering hay, feed and building materials to their many customers since 1981.

Wearing an "eye catching" silver and blue paint scheme, this big powerful Kenworth W900L gets noticed when it is on the road hauling building materials for Holt Transportation of St. George, Utah. New in 2004, #28's drive train includes a 500hp Cat C15 motor with an 18 speed transmission which was spec'd to haul the matched set of Western aluminum Rocky Mountain Double flat bed trailers. The lead trailer is 45 foot long while the rear trailer is 28 feet long. The trailers have super single wheels and tires which help to support the 129,000 pound GVW of the truck when loaded. Western Trailers are manufactured in Boise, Idaho.

Since 1938, Sunroc Corporation has been supplying Utah with quality building materials and building supplies. Sunroc masonry products are manufactured especially for the states of Arizona, Nevada and Utah. A 2005 Navistar Eagle has a full load of split face block on its aluminum 45 foot long main trailer and its 25 foot long pup trailer. The truck is equipped with a 525hp Cummins ISX diesel and a 13 speed transmission.

Super Cubes

Box vans carry dry goods in multiple trailer configuration. They can be refrigerated and carry frozen goods as well as sundries. The majority of American freight moves in box vans.

Cream O'Weber Dairy of Salt Lake City, Utah was founded in Ogden, Utah in 1924 and today serves Utah, Idaho, Colorado and Southeastern Nevada with quality dairy products. An aerodynamic Kenworth T600 pulls a set of "Rocky Mountain Doubles" loaded with fresh milk.

The Coca-Cola bottler in Salt Lake City, Utah supplies products to a distributor in Kingman, Arizona. To deliver these products, sets of Super Double dry box vans are used. A 2004 Freightliner Columbia has a set of 48 foot long and 42 foot long trailers in tow. The Columbia has a 400hp Cat diesel with a 13 speed transmission which enables the driver to manage the 1208 mile long round trip journey with ease.

In order to keep their stores stocked full of merchandise, Walmart, the nation's largest retailer operates one of the largest logistics fleets in the country with over 7,100 truck tractors. Having picked up its twin 45 foot long box trailers, which were loaded at Walmart's distribution center near St. George, Utah, a 2005 Navistar 9400i Eagle is on its way to its delivery destination. #5-0570 has a 435hp Cummins ISX diesel, a 10 speed transmission and 40,000 pound rear ends.

Founded in 1940, Associated Food Stores is an independent wholesale grocery distributor that serves over 600 independent supermarket owners in 8 Intermountain States. Today they ship more than 750 truckloads of grocery products a week from their warehouse in Salt Lake City. A 2005 Volvo VN pulls two refrigerated trailers. The first trailer is 45 foot long while the rear trailer is 42 foot long. The Volvo has a Cummins diesel and a 10 speed transmission.

LTL Triples

Common freight carriers hauling LTL, less that truck load, freight utilize consists that include three 28 foot trailers pulled by the truck tractor and joined together with two trailer dollies which allow them to haul more freight, more economically.

Con-Way Freight #524-6016 has just assembled a matched set of three 28 foot Road Systems Inc. dry box vans. #524-6016 is a 2006 Sterling road tractor that is equipped with a Detroit Diesel power plant, a 10 speed transmission and a tandem "screw" rear end. Con-Way Freight is one of the nation's largest LTL, less than truckload, carriers. They operate 8400 road tractors, 25,000 trailers and serve North America with over 440 operating locations. Road Systems Inc. has been manufacturing trailers from their Searcy, Arkansas facility since 1977. RSI is a division of Con-Way Freight Systems.

This set of triple 28 foot trailers carries LTL, less-than-truckload, freight for ABF Freight System Inc. A new Sterling single axle road tractor equipped with a Mercedes diesel and a 10 speed transmission will pull the "Triples" north into Utah. ABF Freight System Inc. was founded in Fort Smith, Arkansas in 1923 as a local freight carrier. Today, ABF Freight System operates 1600 road truck tractors and over 17,000 28 foot long pup trailers. ABF, Arkansas Best Freight, serves all 50 states and Canada and is one of North America's largest LTL common freight carriers.

Utilizing a fleet of more than 94,000 vehicles, United Parcel Service delivers over 15 million packages a day worldwide. In North America, UPS utilizes 6300 road tractors and 22,000 road trailers to forward parcel packages to more than 215 distribution facilities. UPS #261770, a MACK CH pulls a set of triple 28 foot trailers. UPS refers to their truck with trailer combinations as "feeders". #261770 has a 355hp Mack E6 diesel, a 9 speed transmission and a tandem "screw" rear end. Because this Bulldog is set up to operate in the mountainous Western United States, it is also equipped with an engine exhaust brake. UPS was founded in 1907 in Seattle, Washington as American Messenger Company and in a little more than 100 years has become a world leader in parcel package delivery.

A brand new Navistar 9400 road truck tractor wears the new all orange paint scheme that USF Reddaway Freight has adopted for their road fleet. Truck #8-1478 pulls a set of triples and is equipped with a 435hp Cummins ISX diesel and a 10 speed transmission. Founded in Clackamas, Oregon in 1919, USF Reddaway has been serving the Pacific Northwest for over 90 years. They operate 2300 road truck tractors and 7700 trailers. USF Reddway is a division of YRC, Yellow Roadway Corporation.

OVERSIZE in Miniature

The interest in the real machinery often translates into a desire to own miniatures of the real trucks and equipment. This often starts out while we are children when we get a "toy" to play with. Many companies who produce the real life equipment often have promotional models made to build brand name recognition and to use as sales incentives. The hobby of collecting has grown over the years with more detailed models being produced. There have been thousands of models made by many different manufacturers in many different scales. This chapter highlights a few of the many models produced along with some super detailed custom models produced by enthusiasts.

This exquisite handbuilt model represents Malbro's Autocar prime mover nicknamed "Brutus". The real truck was originally built by them using a Crane Carrier Corp. (CCC) cement mixer from New York City. The mixer and cab were stripped off and the Autocar was built from the frame up. It was designed to and built to do one thing, move big loads and was often called in to finish jobs where other trucks had failed.
The model itselt was scratch built by Dave Natale in 1:25 scale (38 inches long) using plastic, metal and resin castings. The model has aluminum I beam frame rails, metal tubular front axle and solid mount walking beam rear suspension with planetary axles. The cab is a resin castimg from A.I.T.M. and the hood, grill and fenders are all scratch built from Evergreen plastic. It has a Caterpillar 3408 diesel engine with a 16 speed transmission. The Rogers 125 ton I bearm trailer was also completely scratch built using plastic, metal and resin castings. The goose neck and rear axle unit detach from the beam for loading. *(Photo courtesy of Dave Natale)*

The history of oversized truck models is long and these are a few examples. The old models were made as toys for children, not as highly detailed miniatures that are currently made as promotional or collectors items now. The technology in creating models has changed over the years just as the technology for building the real prototypes has evolved. Although the older toys are simpler, they most certainly do not lack in character.

Left: This Pacific transporter model was made by France Jouets of France in the mid 1960's. This is 1:43 scale and was a fantastic toy for the time with a working winch to hold down the transformers.

Right: The Scammel was a British truck model and is seen here pulling a 200 ton super heavy haul trailer with a Ruston-Bucyrus 22-RB shovel. This model was made in the 1960's by Lesney (Matchbox) in England. This model is approximately 1:87 scale.

Below: This heavy haul combination was limited edition of 50 sets produced by Trainscapes in 1:87 scale. The Mack truck tractor is a modified model made by Herpa of Germany. The lowbed trailer was custom made for the set. The Cat quarry truck was made by Shinsei of Japan.

This 1:50 scale example of a Cline Isco 240C truck tractor is a pulling a 100 ton trailer loaded with a scale model of a Cat D9H dozer. This model was produced by Engineering Model Developments (EMD) as a "handbuilt" model. Most handbuilts are limited runs of less than 100 models produced. The truck is primarily resin with white metal and brass detail parts. *(Photo courtesy of Buffalo Road Imports)*

Smith models of England produced a variety of handbuilt models of American and European prototypes in 1:48 scale out of white metal. The International Eagle pulling the trailer is a 10 axle combination hauling a 1:50 scale model of an SMIT transformer produced by WSI Models. *(Photo courtesy of Buffalo Road Imports)*

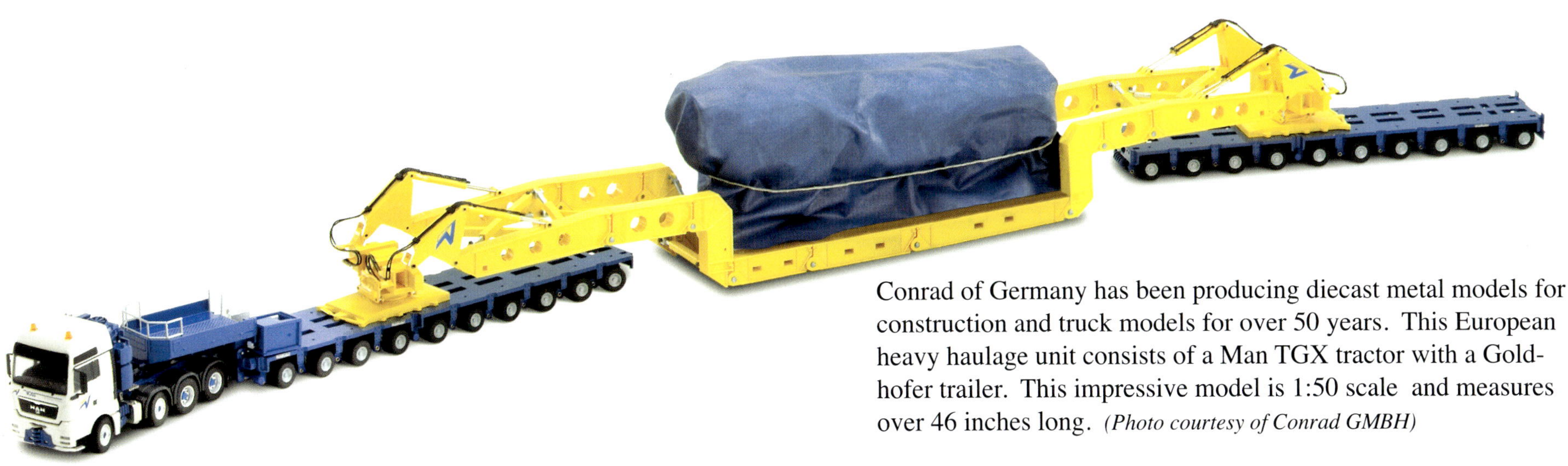

Conrad of Germany has been producing diecast metal models for construction and truck models for over 50 years. This European heavy haulage unit consists of a Man TGX tractor with a Goldhofer trailer. This impressive model is 1:50 scale and measures over 46 inches long. *(Photo courtesy of Conrad GMBH)*

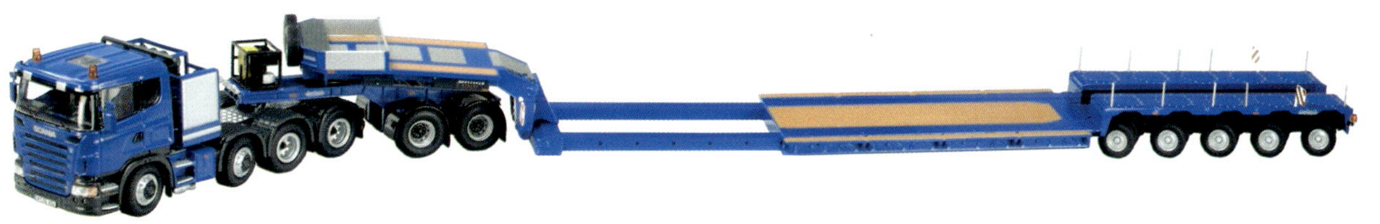

NZG is another Nurnberg, Germany based manufacturer of diecast metal models. Although the headquarters is still located in Germany, production has been moved to China. This model represents a Scania R 8x4 tractor with a Nooteboom extendable trailer. This model is 1:50 and is 21 inches long and can be extended to just over 25 inches long. *(Photo courtesy of NZG Modelle)*

The Cat 784C tractor pulls a Towhaul lowbed. These units are made for moving oversized machinery within mines. This model is 1:50 scale and is over 25 inches long. This monstrous diecast model is made by Norscot. *(Photo courtesy of Norscot)*

This "OVERSIZE" super haul unit was made by All World Models. This very limited edition model of only 100 units of a Contractors Cargo Company super haul unit is 1:87 scale (HO gauge trains) and 24 inches long. The Kenworth trucks and CCC trailer are brass with the vacuum vessel made from plexiglass and plastruct. *(Photo courtesy of Ralph Johnson of All World Models)*

The Peterbilt 379 pulls a 3 axle Talbert trailer with an additional "flip" axle. These models are 1:87 scale and are another prime example of how finer detail can be obtained in brass. These brass models are limited run models made by Classic Mint Collectibles. The load is a Komatsu PC400 excavator with a LaBounty shear. These models were sold separately with very limited quantities produced. *(Photo courtesy of Buffalo Road Imports)*

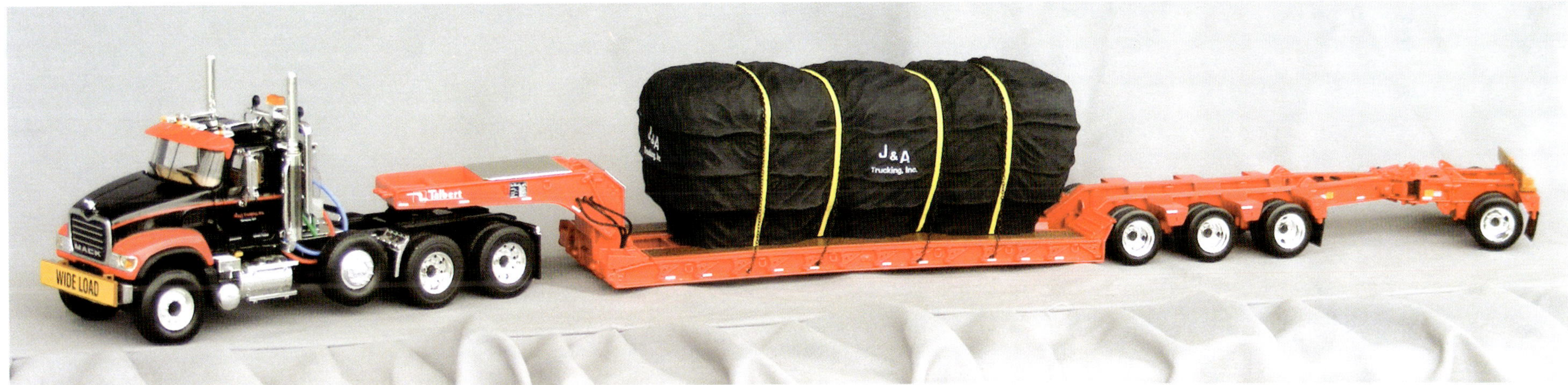

Top: Tonkin produces a range of diecast metal trucks in 1:53 scale including this Kenworth pulling an XL lowbed trailer. The load is a Komatsu D65 bulldozer produced by Universal Hobbies. *(Photo courtesy of Buffalo Road Imports)*

Middle: The J&A Trucking Mack Granite truck tractor pulling a Talbert flip axle trailer was made by First Gear as a limited run model. First Gear produces mostly 1:34 and 1:50 scale trucks. *(Photo courtesy of Buffalo Road Imports)*

Bottom: Gerosa was a famous name on the East Coast for heavy haulage. Corgi Models produced this model in 1:50 scale of a Diamond T prime mover pulling the 6 axle heavy haul trailer.

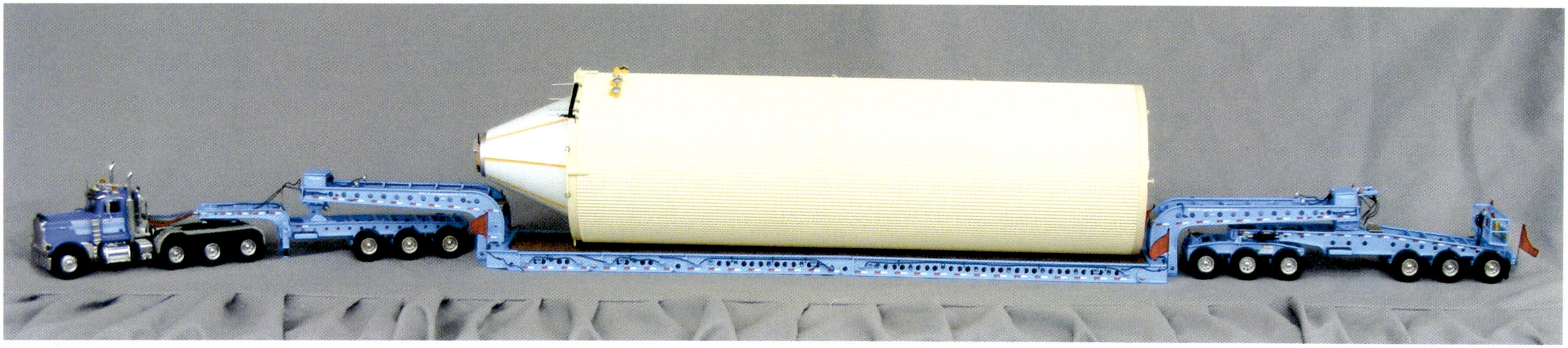

Above: The Peterbilt 379 with the Nelson 3x3x3 trailer is 1:50 scale diecast model by Sword Models. The model measures 42 inches long was made in 6 different colors. *(Photo courtesy of Buffalo Road Imports)*

Right: Herpa of Germany has been producing 1:87 scale trucks in plastic for many years. This unit consists of 2 Mercedes tractors with a Goldhofer trailer carrying a bridge bed. *(Photo courtesy of Buffalo Road Imports)*

Right: The Faun prime mover and Scheurle heavy transport trailer is a built up Kibri plastic kit. Kibri produces are large line of highly detailed models of heavy commercial vehicles and construction equipment machinery in 1:87 scale for HO train modelers. *(Photo courtesy of Buffalo Road Imports)*

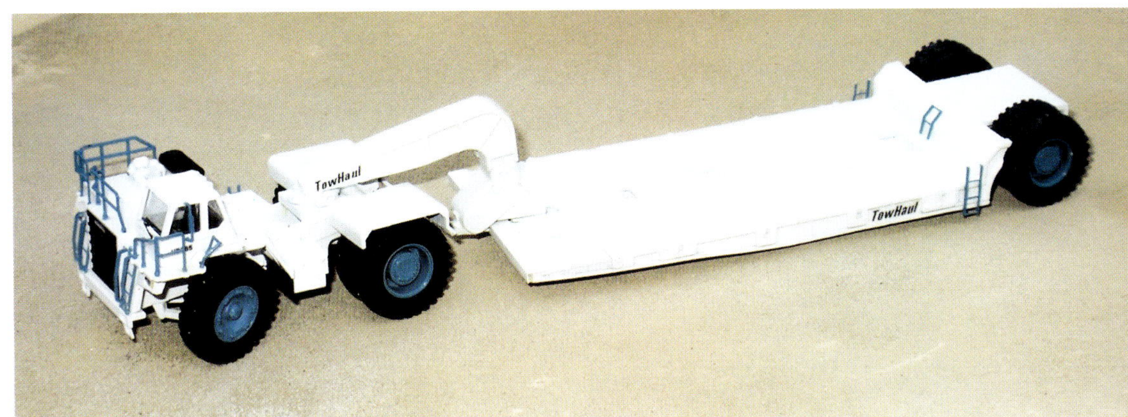

Left: This model is a custom model built by Wayne Calder. The tractor unit is a modified Komatsu HD785 mine truck made by Kibri. The trailer was "kit bashed" and represents a typical 200 ton TowHaul trailer. The model is 1:87 scale and measures 12.25 inches long. *(Photo courtesy of Wayne Calder)*

Below: This custom model was built by Mark Wayman in 1:87 scale. The Autocar prime movers are kit bashed using Lee Town cabs and the platform trailer is a Scheurle made by Kibri Models.

Left: This impressive model of a Gerosa heavy haul unit made by Edward J. Sweeney is 1:87 scale. This unit consists of an Autocar AP19 tractor pulling a 350 ton Rogers low-boy. This model was completely scratch built except for the truck cab and the trailer tires. *(Photo courtesy of Edward J. Sweeney)*

Right: This Kenworth 953 is a highly detailed resin model from Romania. It is built by Dan's Models, formerly known as Miniatur Models, SRL. These are all handbuilt models in very limited quantity. *(Photo courtesy of Buffalo Road Imports)*

This true to life 1:24 scale model of Hallamore's prime mover #330, a Mack M-45SX, was constructed 95% from scratch, meaning that with the exception of the sear, air horns & lights, everything was made by hand for this model. Richard C. Mark who built the model worked from drawings obtained from Mack Trucks Inc. and photographs of the actual truck. Every detail was reproduced from the Cummins VT-1710 engine and Allison CLBT-5960 transmission to the Mack Plani-Drive rear axles. The tires were patterned in ABS then cast in molds for multiple parts. From start to finish. the model took 6 weeks to build. *(Photos courtesy of Richard C. Mark, Industrial Model Development)*

Shows & Events

Enthusiasts have also enjoyed getting together to meet other collectors and enthusiasts, buy new models for their collections or just see new models they have not seen. These shows offer a fun time for all those who attend.

The largest show in the world for trucks and construction equipment models is Model Show Europe which is held in the Netherlands each year. In the United States, the IMCATS show (International Model Construction & Truck Show) held in Clarence, New York offers a large variety of truck and construction equipment models. These shows offer working models, custom built models and a large selection of models for sale. More information on these shows can be found on their web sites:

www.modelshow-europe.com

www.imcats.com

There are two major shows put on within the United States each year on the real trucks and equipment. The American Truck Historical Society (ATHS) sponsors a national show for trucks and the Historical Construction Equipment Association (HCEA) sponsors a national show for vintage equipment. Each club has regional chapters that also sponsor smaller shows

The pictures on this page are from the IMCATS show (International Model Construction and Truck Show) that is held annually in Clarence, New York. The show consists of displays of dioramas, static models and working models along with prototypes of new models from manufacturers and also thousands of models for sale.

Buffalo Road Imports (BRI) has been officially serving the collector since 1978. Business was initially started by exhibiting at toy shows and as a small mail order business that was an off shoot from collecting. Although BRI specializes in construction scale models, many other types of collectible vehicles, trucks, soldiers, ships and more are stocked. Being a collector as well, Brandon Lewis, owner of BRI, is considered one of the leading experts in the field of construction scale models.

The business officially began in 1978 with the purchase of the remaining stock of the US importer for NZG & Conrad. Soon thereafter, the first shipments started to arrive from Europe with construction scale models. The family business grew slowly while Brandon attended college for engineering. Fortunately for collectors, when he graduated with a degree in petroleum engineering in 1982, the oil market was extremely slow and unable to find a job in the engineering field, he worked in the family business. During this time BRI expanded by carrying more manufacturer lines to offer the largest selection of construction scale models worldwide. In 1991, BRI moved to its current home in Clarence, NY and opened a retail shop which displays over 10,000 models of construction, military, soldiers, cars, trucks, buses, airplanes and trains. The shop draws visitors from all over the world.

The year 1988 was a big year with the initial startup of EMD (Engineering Model Developments). This is a sister company for the production of models. The first model was of the Caterpillar D8-R crawler tractor with a Hyster winch and logging arch.

With the increased interest in construction and truck scale models, BRI sponsored the first annual International Model Construction and Truck Show (IMCATS) in Clarence, NY in 2004. This allowed fellow construction and truck enthusiasts in the US and worldwide to come and see thousands of scale models on display and for sale from manufacturers, dealers and customizers.

BRI continues to serve the collectors and enthusiasts and is proud to publish this book and possible future interesting titles for you.

Informational Web Sites

The following web sites are great sources of additional information.

American Truck Historical Society:	www.aths.org
Hank's Truck Pictures:	www.hankstruckpictures.com
Historical Construction Equipment Assn.:	www.hcea.net
1/87 Vehicle Club:	www.1-87vehicles.org

A 80 foot long precast concrete pipe rides behind Quality Towing's big Freightliner "Classic XL". The front end of the precast pipe is riding on a 16 tire Cozad jeep while the rear sits on a 32 tire Cozad self steering dolly. Quality removed the 24 foot long deck from their Cozad 2+2+2 heavy haul lowbed trailer so that they could utilize the jeep and dolly in this specialized transport manner. Quality Towing's truck #72 has a 500hp Cat 3406E diesel, an 18 speed transmission and 46,000 pound rear ends. The bright green heavy haul jeep and dolly were fabricated and assembled in Stockton, California at Cozad Trailers' manufacturing facility.

About the Author:

Mark Wayman grew up in Northern Arizona where as a young boy he was fascinated by the trains that traveled through downtown Flagstaff. Watching and later photographing the Santa Fe Railway would become one of his favorite pastimes.

Growing up in Arizona also exposed him to the massive equipment that was used to mine copper and the heavy lift cranes that were used to assemble these machines that had been transported in on railroad flat cars and on big heavy haul trucks with lowbed trailers.

(Photo by S. L. Peters)

For nearly 40 years Mark has been photo documenting trains, cranes and heavy construction and mining equipment. Mark learned about photography from his father, Kenneth, who was a reporter for a local newspaper. Not only did Mark learn how to use a twin lens reflex camera, he also learned dark room procedures as well as how to set type, load newsprint and sweep the floor. To this day one of Mark's most prized possessions is his father's Mamiya C330 twin reflex lens camera.

Whenever Mark traveled to Phoenix his first stop was always at the Reliance Crane and Rigging yard to visit Cecil Pelts, who always had time to talk to Mark and answer his many questions. Mark was allowed to roam the facility and photograph the trucks, cranes and heavy haul prime movers. It was here that he first encountered what he still believes to be the most impressive heavy haul road truck tractors that he ever saw, Reliance Truck's R model Mack Westerns. Reliance built these 240 inch long wheel base trucks from glider kits which included 335 Cummins diesels and 15 speed transmissions with 4 speed brownies and Budd wheels. It would not be until later in life that he would learn from East Coast friends that only West Coast Mack trucks had Budds.

While growing up Mark's life was not only influenced by working for his father but also by John Kroll, George Fornara and Fred Smith who taught him that hard work was not an option in life, it is a way of life.

Mark still enjoys photo documenting cranes, heavy construction equipment, mining equipment, heavy trucks and an occasional tug boat. He also notes that over the years many, many makes and models of trucks, construction equipment and cranes have disappeared due to mergers, buy outs and global consolidation. He feels most fortunate to have been able to see them and photograph them before they disappeared.

Mark has a wonderful wife, Terri Sue, who has been both supportive and patient with his hobby and this endeavor. He resides in Las Vegas, Nevada with his 3 four legged children, Shasta Akita, Buddy Lee Lasso and Elvis Pinscher.

This is his first book.

Mark's Blessings:

Terri Sue Wayman
Anna Wayman Trujillo
Sherrie Wayman Hanna
Keith Wayman

Brayden Michael
Blas Roberto
Collin Dean
Aemelio Enrique
Kelsey Taylor
Keirsten Sue

Index